FOR JOSS,
AND OUR THREE BEAUTIFUL BOYS,
GEORGE, ALFIE AND WILLIAM

KITCHEN
by Mike

K

MIKE McENEARNEY

PHOTOGRAPHY BY ALAN BENSON

LANTERN

an imprint of
PENGUIN BOOKS

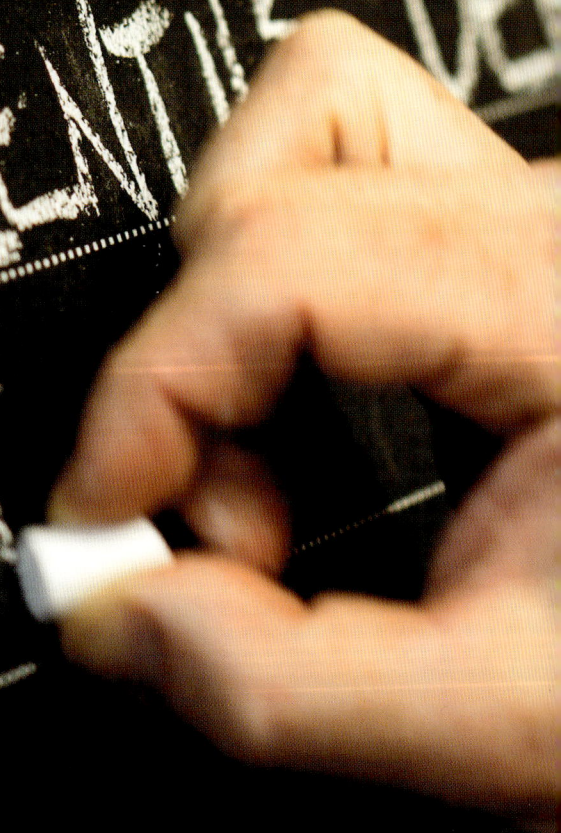

FOREWORD

In the early 1990s a young man walked into my kitchen at Rockpool. Clean-cut and eager, he looked more marine than cook. From that first day, I could tell he wasn't in a hurry, but was on a mission to do the best he could, and to get the best out of himself. It was clear that he knew what he wanted.

Mike McEnearney was a good student of cooking. Inquisitive, forthright and hard-working, he was just the type of young cook I loved having in my kitchen. He spent several years with me, working his way up the totem pole, covering each section – larder, fish, meat, pasta and sauce – and calling service. He excelled in each, not only becoming a very good cook, but a person who could relate to and manage others and take on the responsibility of running a kitchen. Young Michael had come a long way in a few short years.

Mike left Rockpool to travel overseas, but we never lost contact and I followed his adventures with interest, always catching up with him when in England. He grew into a fine chef, running restaurants in London and learning an immense amount about food and what he loves so much now: the four seasons that Europe has to offer, where spring, summer, autumn and winter influence the palette of cooking so strongly. He also met the beautiful Joss, who would become his wife, and had three gorgeous boys – a very important part of who Mike is today.

When, in 2006, he said he wanted to come back to Australia and give the family a taste of Sydney life, I jumped at the chance to have him back at Rockpool, this time in the capacity of executive chef. Mike didn't let me down, and for 3 years led the team with great authority and consistency.

He subsequently left in 2009 to travel, exploring more of Europe and living sustainably on a farm in Wales, before realising that Sydney was the place for him and his family to settle once and for all. After a short stint at Iggy's, one of Sydney's great bread-bakers, he was ready to open his own place, just as he'd dreamed of all those years ago. He had formed an opinion that it didn't have to be grand – as a matter of fact, it was to be the very opposite of the restaurants where he had worked most of his life. It was to be the same as the man: forthright and simple, but breathtakingly beautiful because of that very simplicity. This was to be cooking not only of the season, but of the day; the best in the market would be at Kitchen by Mike. Is it a restaurant, canteen or delicatessen? It really doesn't matter, because what it is is an expression of Mike's beautiful food in a rustic and informal room that screams sustainable, delicious food.

The same food that is in Mike's extraordinary kitchen is on the pages of this book. I know you will all want to taste whatever you see, and that it will have you cooking the recipes immediately.

I feel proud to know Mike – the man, his family, his kitchen and now his book – and wonderfully proud to have had some very small part in helping him on his journey.

NEIL PERRY

INTRODUCTION

Life is made up of separate chapters.

As a child, no single experience drew me to food. That came a little later. I grew up in the north-western suburbs of Sydney, eating Vegemite sandwiches from my school lunchbox and grilled meat with lumpy mashed potato for dinner. On Thursdays, after late-night shopping, we'd often get takeaway, such as McDonald's, and on the weekends we'd sit down to mum's roast lamb or spag bol. This all seemed very commonplace during the late 1970s and early '80s. Food just wasn't on my radar.

But by the time I had finished high school, I was spending much of my spare time in the city with friends, and this was where the penny dropped. I was seeing and tasting new things: I loved eating plates of roast duck and Chinese greens at BBQ King before going to a club, or buying wonderful olives and sliced meats from Cyril's Deli before meeting friends for a picnic in the Botanical Gardens. At 18, I had developed a serious interest in food. The obvious next step was a chef apprenticeship, and when an opening came up at Neil Perry's fledgling Rockpool, I really landed on my feet. I truly believe that your early experiences in the kitchen shape the chef you will become. Neil became my mentor, and he was responsible for igniting my passion for food.

Then, at the age of 24, I embarked on the extended trip around Europe that is virtually a rite of passage for curious Australians. What started as a twelve-month holiday grew into a ten-year food odyssey. I flooded my mind and tastebuds with new experiences; I loved the different cultures, and history that I could immerse myself in at the click of a Eurostar ticket; but most of all, I loved the seasons. They became a framework for my cooking – asparagus in spring, strawberries around the time of Wimbledon, 'the glorious twelfth' of August that heralded the start of the game season, and the wild mushrooms of autumn. This respect for the seasons has informed everything I have done since.

During my time in London, I worked the stoves of some of the city's finest restaurants. After stints at the Michelin-starred Pied à Terre with Tom Aikens at the helm, and then at Sir Terence Conran's Mezzo and Bluebird, in 1997 I was headhunted by Damien Hirst's trail-blazing Pharmacy restaurant and art installation. With a celebrity-studded clientele that included Joe Strummer, Harold Pinter, Hugh Grant and Nigella Lawson, not only did Pharmacy plunge me into the London scene, it also led me to my future wife, Joss Best, who worked front of house. These were fun years – our motto was work hard, play hard. In between work and nightclubs, I frequented Borough Market, where Neal's Yard Dairy and The Ginger Pig were spearheading the renaissance of artisanal British food. When Pharmacy was sold, I ran the kitchens at a handful of high-profile restaurants, among them the venerable Scott's, in Mayfair, and Oliver Peyton's award-winning Inn the Park.

By 2006 Joss and I had a young family, and Australia, land of blue skies and beachside living, was beckoning us. With Rockpool Bar & Grill opening in Melbourne, Neil Perry was looking for someone to head the kitchen at his flagship Sydney restaurant. Returning to Rockpool as executive chef was incredible: after ten years of amazing European food experiences, I was so proud to be back where it had all begun for me. I felt as if I had come full circle.

// IT WAS TIME TO MAKE MY OWN DREAMS COME TRUE.

When 2010 came around, I realised that I had been cooking for 20 years in some of the top restaurants in the world – but what I yearned for was something much simpler, without all the trappings of fine dining.

I have always loved great bread, and when I was executive chef of Rockpool, I had become good friends with Igor and Ludmilla of Iggy's Bread of the World, in Bronte. Living close to their bakery, I would often wake to the smell of amazing bread; they generously took me under their wing and allowed me to learn from a master of the craft. My time there was one of the turning points in my career, as my focus shifted to understanding how such basic ingredients as flour, water and salt could be transformed into something that to me is a work of art.

After nearly a year of baking at Iggy's, the need to cook as well as bake returned. My wife Joss put it very plainly: 'Mike, you don't need a big fancy restaurant. All you need is a stove to cook on, and a table to eat from.' Such clarity! She was absolutely right, of course. All I wanted to do was cook. As soon as I realised I didn't need the million-dollar fit-out, I could think outside the box. And once I did that, there was no box. All that mattered was the food and the people enjoying it.

As luck would have it, I found one of the most charming spaces in all of Sydney for my return to the stoves. The result was a year-long series of pop-up dinners at my friend Andrew Forst's French-chic antiques and interiors showroom in Surry Hills, ici et la. While Andrew made napkins from striped-canvas offcuts of his signature deckchairs, I borrowed plates from friends and brought in the beautiful silver cutlery my grandmother had given me. Mike's Table took the format of a five-course seasonal set dinner offered on alternate Sundays – a moveable feast for 42 people. There was no kitchen; every fortnight, I had to hire a three-ring gas burner and a small oven, along with two trestle tables. I would visit the markets and base the menu on what I found there. It was totally off the cuff, and it was totally exciting.

Through Igor and Ludmilla, I learnt that the forward-thinking Russel Koskela and Sasha Titchkosky of the Koskela design team had taken over a vast factory site in Rosebery. I didn't even know where Rosebery was. All I'd heard was that its wide, tree-lined and relatively traffic-free side streets were where you went as a learner to practise your reverse parking! But, at our very first site visit and meeting, we hit it off, and a partnership was born. Originally a factory for the Rosella soup company in 1913, the building had lain empty for quite some time and was little more than a shell. It was filthy, but had great bones: exposed beams and brickwork, enormous windows and a roller door.

Wondering how to approach such an imposing space, I kept returning to the fact that this had been built as a factory, and a factory always has its staff canteen. The more I thought about it, the more the canteen model felt right. This would be food for the people, with no bias to any demographic. Everyone would be treated the same way: rich man, poor man, student, lawyer, all in the same queue. This paring back would make space for deeply considered cooking, and the opportunity to showcase some of the country's finest food producers at reasonable prices. I wanted to strip away the trappings of traditional restaurant dining to find something more basic and perhaps more honest. It was time to get real.

Once we had the keys, it took us just over six months to open. The design brief was simple: a large display bench for the food, set in front of an open kitchen that was powered by a wood-fired oven. Russel and Sasha got it exactly right, coming up with a design sympathetic to the space. Outside, recycled packing crates were transformed into a deck, while inside it was all exposed brick and concrete, and the distinctive Jake chairs that have become a Kitchen by Mike signature. So the scene was set, but would people want to line up for their food and eat off tin plates? It was a risk I was keen to take.

5

// THIS WAS WHEN THE KITCHEN BY MIKE CHAPTER OF MY LIFE BEGAN.

6

On our first day, 12 February 2012, we opened to a queue that hasn't stopped since. It was only when we were about to swing open the doors at 7 a.m. that we realised we didn't have anything to put the cutlery in! I turned to see pizza sauce being made in the kitchen with tins of San Marzano tomatoes. I carefully pulled the label off an empty tin, washed the tin and stuck the label back on. Those cutlery tins in the middle of each table have since become a metaphor for what Kitchen by Mike is all about: improvisation, spontaneity and sharing.

Our days begin at 4 a.m., when whoever is baking for the day takes the sourdough out of the fridge and fires up the oven. It takes all five senses to adjust the environment of the living sourdough, and even then the twenty loaves we bake daily are never exactly the same – that's what makes them special. When the rest of the kitchen staff roll in the door with a yawn at 6 a.m., our baker has already baked muffins and pastries, cakes and tarts and is about to score the first loaves before they go into the oven. The kitchen crew gather and toss around menu ideas and prep lists before they start the day with coffee. The menu is never really set in stone; it is merely a tentative list of dishes we want to cook that day with the produce we have available. My frequent visits to the markets mean that I get to keep my finger on the pulse, buy what is in season and of course what is well-priced.

When I turn up at 7.30 a.m. with a carload of produce, the chefs are quite often faced with things they have never seen before, and of a quality that's inspiring. This is one of the most rewarding things about Kitchen by Mike. I am surrounded by passionate and capable people who enable me to serve honest and responsible food. We use quirks to our advantage, thriving on flexibility and allowing things to take shape organically. The only rules are that the food is seasonal, and is sourced and cooked with integrity. To this end, we maintain close relationships with our producers, many of them small and local. We seek beauty in imperfection, as opposed to the bland and standardised offerings of the supermarkets.

The floor staff arrive between 6.30 and 8 a.m., and are kept busy serving breakfast, making coffee, polishing glasses, watering the garden, juicing, writing labels, receiving deliveries and posting the day's menu on Facebook.

By 11.30 a.m. the lunchtime queue is already building. The lunch menu is chalked up on the board and the counter is scrubbed and ready: there are always two meat or fish dishes straight from the oven, six different salads, sourdough wood-fired pizza, assorted rolls, wraps, quiches and tartines. Not to mention the cakes, biscuits and pastries alongside the handmade cordials and juices.

Right on 12 noon, the lunch service begins. It is a canteen, remember, so you wait your turn, then point to whatever you want; everything is individually priced, so you just choose what you like and pay at the till. The counter is constantly replenished with food made fresh by the kitchen in full view, which reassures people that what they are getting is at its peak. A platter rarely lasts more than ten minutes before a new one replaces it.

I love serving the food at lunch and getting to know the regulars. Some come two or three times a day, others less often, but it is our love for food that brings us together. The banter over the servery reveals interests in common, and gives me a sense of what works and what doesn't. It also gives me the chance to talk about the produce, who grows it and other good ways to cook it – it's all about sharing the experience.

Lunch is over by 3 p.m., and afternoon tea is served until 4 p.m., when we close the doors ready to do it all again tomorrow.

To truly experience Kitchen by Mike, you have to visit it. I hope this book encourages those who have not yet been to come, and delights those who have already lined up on so many occasions.

HOW TO USE THIS BOOK

As you may have noticed, I am obsessed with the seasons.

Cooking what's in season is better for you – nutritionally and ethically. I don't want my kids to eat food that is pumped full of chemicals to make it grow, nor flown halfway around the world at all times of the year. The bottom line for me is that it's all about flavour. Food in season just tastes better . . . the flavour is in its prime. Since time began, people have been living in accordance with the seasons and with nature. Right now, with the economic and geographical climates in peril, we have begun to realise the importance of respecting the seasons – and in the process, are discovering a simpler, ultimately richer way of life. Waiting for the arrival of each season is like waiting for a birthday – it only comes once a year, so you really look forward to it and enjoy every moment when it's here.

Arranged by season, the recipes range from breakfast, through to salads, more substantial dishes and sweet offerings. Many of them are simple and take minutes to prepare; others are broken up into a number of stages to fit in with our busy lives.

At the back of the book is a 'Larder' section, to inspire you to make the most of what's plentiful each season – and give you a head start in the kitchen. Having a well-stocked larder is a saviour in so many ways. Not only will it halve your cooking time, but it will also save you a fortune because you will have preserved ingredients when they were at their best and their cheapest.

If stored correctly, many of these preparations have a long shelf-life and are invaluable for adding flair to your daily cooking. A great example is the black bean vinaigrette on page 231. Simply cut an avocado in half, remove the seed and fill the cavity with the vinaigrette – job done! Or serve it as a dipping sauce with slices of raw fish or toss a few spoonfuls through a stir-fry. You'll notice that a lot of the recipes cross-reference each other, and I hope this will encourage you to try other combinations.

This book is a snapshot of a year at Kitchen by Mike.

CHAPTER

SPR1

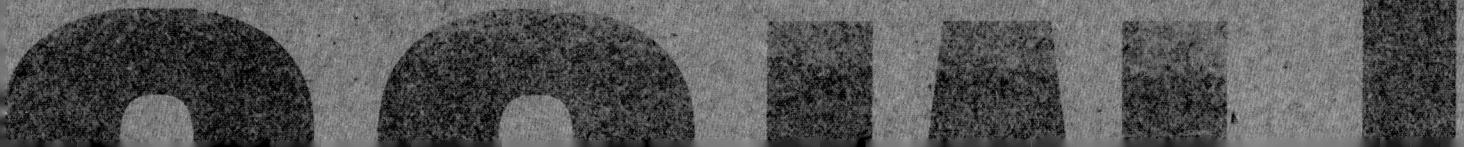

12

BLOOD ORANGE & CAMPARI CLUTCH START

SERVES 4

25 g caster sugar
500 ml blood orange juice (from about 10 blood oranges)
100 ml Campari
ice cubes
4 sprigs rosemary

I love fresh OJ in the morning, particularly with the extra intensity of blood oranges and the earthy flavour of rosemary, infused as you stir in between sips. This vibrant drink is the perfect hair of the dog when you rise from your slumber after a big night. If you're feeling sluggish and need all the help you can get, add a pinch of cayenne pepper to get the blood pumping.

For a heath-boosting blood orange and oregano tonic, replace the Campari with 4 drops of oregano oil (available from health-food stores), which is great for the immune system and helps to purge the body of parasites.

Place the sugar and 25 ml of water in a small saucepan and simmer until the sugar has dissolved. Remove from the heat and leave the syrup to cool.

Place the blood orange juice, Campari and syrup in a cocktail shaker with a handful of ice and shake until combined.

Pour into chilled glasses over more ice and place a long sprig of rosemary in each glass for stirring.

Good morning!

BIRCHER MUESLI WITH STEWED RHUBARB

SERVES 4

200 g rolled oats (not instant)
2 teaspoons chia seeds
juice of 1 lemon
2 granny smith apples
500 g natural yoghurt
150 g honey
40 g hazelnuts

STEWED RHUBARB

500 g rhubarb, cut into
   1 cm chunks
125 g caster sugar
1 vanilla bean, split and
   seeds scraped
juice of ½ lemon, if needed

Bircher muesli is a super start to the day for the warmer months, instead of porridge. It works best if you can do some of the prep in advance: ideally, toss the rhubarb in the sugar the morning of the day before. That evening, cook the rhubarb and soak the oats, then you're all set for a quick and delicious breakfast the next morning.

You should be able to find chia seeds at health-food stores and most supermarkets. This makes about 350 g stewed rhubarb, but it will keep for up to a week in the fridge and is great with yoghurt.

Mix together the oats, chia seeds, lemon juice and 100 ml of water, then leave to soak overnight in the fridge.

For the stewed rhubarb, toss the rhubarb with the sugar in a non-reactive saucepan, then cover and leave to steep overnight at room temperature.

In the morning, simmer the rhubarb and its juices over medium heat with the vanilla for 10 minutes until the rhubarb is tender and starting to break up. Remove from the heat and allow to cool, adding lemon juice to taste if it is too sweet.

Meanwhile, grate the apples and fold through the soaked oats, then stir in the yoghurt and honey.

Spoon the muesli into bowls and top with a dollop of stewed rhubarb and a scattering of hazelnuts.

14

BUBBLE & SQUEAK WITH A FRIED EGG

SERVES 4

3–4 waxy potatoes (about 500 g), peeled and cut into 2 cm chunks

2 small parsnips, peeled and cut into chunks

1 large carrot, peeled and cut into chunks

2 tablespoons duck fat or olive oil

1 onion, roughly chopped

2 garlic cloves, finely chopped

1 bunch cavolo nero, shredded

30 g (¼ cup) peas

1 tablespoon thyme leaves

3 spring onions, sliced

handful of flat-leaf parsley leaves, shredded

salt flakes and freshly ground black pepper

2 tablespoons unsalted butter

4 eggs

Bubble and squeak is all about using up leftover vegetables from the weekend roast, so if you have these, there's no need to start from scratch. Just mix them all together and proceed from the stage where you add the parsley and spring onion. Otherwise, read on.

You can serve any number of things with bubble and squeak. With or without the egg, try it with sauteed spinach, mushrooms, crispy bacon, sausages or even seared duck livers if you're feeling decadent.

Preheat the oven to 250°C.

Boil the potato, parsnip and carrot in salted water until just tender. Drain well.

Heat the duck fat or olive oil in a heavy-based roasting tin. Add the drained vegetables and roast for 10–15 minutes or until golden and crisp. Remove from the tin and set aside. Place the roasting tin over medium heat on the stovetop, add the onion and garlic and saute until soft and translucent. Add the cavolo nero and saute until tender, then add the peas and thyme and gently cook for a minute or so, just to bring the flavours together. Leave to cool slightly.

When the vegetable mixture is cool enough to handle, add the spring onion and most of the parsley and gently mix together, squashing the vegetables to form a lumpy mash. Taste and season with salt and pepper if needed, then form the mash into four patties.

Melt half of the butter in a large frying pan over medium heat and cook the bubble and squeak patties on both sides until golden brown and heated through. Remove and keep warm while you cook the eggs.

Wipe out the frying pan with paper towel, turn the heat up to medium–high and add the remaining butter. Gently crack the eggs into a bowl, then pour them into the hot pan in one go – they will space themselves out. Cook until the whites are just set but the yolks are still runny, then cut in between each egg with an egg flip and lift them out.

Place the bubble and squeak patties on warm plates, top each one with an egg, scatter with the remaining shredded parsley and serve immediately.

16

PEA & HAM SOUP

SERVES 4

250 g dried split peas

pinch of bicarbonate of soda

25 ml extra virgin olive oil

1 small carrot, finely chopped

1 celery stick, finely chopped

1 small onion, finely chopped

2 garlic cloves, finely chopped

1 smoked ham hock

1 bay leaf

salt flakes and freshly ground white pepper

1 tablespoon thyme leaves

This is a wonderful hearty soup that you can leave cooking away happily and not have to give too much attention. It's great with just grilled bread and olive oil, or mix it up a little and serve it with pasta or grains, such as barley or freekeh.

All you need to remember is to soak the split peas overnight to flush out any impurities and help them cook more evenly. As for the smoked hock, not all butchers stock it, so it's a good idea to order in advance – you can always pop it in the freezer until the day comes when you want to make some soup.

Soak the split peas overnight in 1 litre (4 cups) of water with the bicarbonate of soda.

The next day, drain the split peas and rinse well, then tie one third of them in a loose muslin (or clean Chux cloth) bundle, leaving plenty of space for them to expand as they cook.

Heat the olive oil in a flameproof casserole or heavy-based saucepan over medium heat, add the carrot, celery, onion and garlic and saute until soft and starting to caramelise, about 10 minutes.

Add the other two-thirds of the split peas, plus the ham hock, bay leaf and 1 litre (4 cups) of water. Season with a pinch of salt and a couple of grindings of white pepper, then bring to the boil, skimming off any foam that forms on the surface, and simmer gently for 2½ hours.

Remove the muslin bag of peas and the ham hock. When the ham hock is cool enough to handle, remove the fat, skin and meat. Reserve about ½ cup of the fat and skin, but discard the bone. Tear the meat into bite-sized pieces.

Puree the soup with the reserved fat and skin from the ham hock. You can use a food processor or a stick blender for this, but it is important to break up the fat and skin so its presence enriches the soup, yet is not unpleasant to chew on.

Stir the meat back into the soup, along with the peas from the muslin bag, and bring to the boil. Taste and adjust the seasoning if necessary. If the soup is too thick, thin it down with a little water.

Ladle the soup into bowls and scatter the thyme leaves over the top.

18

BOUILLABAISSE WITH ROUILLE & CROUTONS

SERVES 8

4 × 250–300 g red mullet, filleted

4 × 350–400 g john dory, filleted

4 × 400–500 g bream, filleted

22 garlic cloves, 8 left whole,
    12 finely chopped and 2 bruised

large pinch of salt flakes

120 ml extra virgin olive oil

2 blue swimmer crabs,
    thawed if frozen

2 teaspoons fennel seeds

125 ml (½ cup) white wine

1 small onion, finely chopped

1 red capsicum (pepper),
    finely chopped

1 small carrot, finely chopped

2 small celery sticks, finely chopped

2 small fennel bulbs, trimmed and
    finely chopped, fronds reserved

4 vine-ripened tomatoes, chopped

650 g redfish, gutted, cleaned and
    chopped (ask your fishmonger
    to do this)

500 ml (2 cups) fish stock
    (see page 242)

800 g kipfler potatoes, scrubbed

large pinch of saffron threads

freshly ground black pepper

generous squeeze of lemon juice

≥

Bouillabaisse is a grand soup that's just perfect for a hands-on lunch with friends. Traditionally, it is made with several different kinds of fish, chosen for their diverse flavours and textures, but if your choice is limited, just use more of whatever fish is available. Instead of fish filleted by your friendly fishmonger, you could use whole fish if you prefer – just increase the baking time to 15 minutes.

If you want to get a head start, you can make the stock in advance and keep it in the fridge for up to 3 days or in the freezer for 3 months.

The rouille will keep for 3 days in the fridge, and any leftovers are delicious as a dip for crudites or spread on a sandwich with crab and prawns. I also love it for dunking chips into instead of mayo. Using fish liver in the rouille is optional, but it does give the sauce a strong flavour of the sea, which I love, as well as intensifying the taste of the soup when the rouille is added. Ask your fishmonger to keep some when filleting the fish – ordering in advance is advisable.

Lay the fish fillets on a large plate. Crush the whole garlic cloves with the salt and combine with 80 ml (⅓ cup) olive oil. Smear this garlic-infused oil over the fish and leave to marinate in the fridge while you make the bouillabaisse and rouille.

Preheat the oven to 200°C. Crack the crabs and chop into 3 cm pieces. Toss with the fennel seeds and 20 ml olive oil in a small roasting tin and roast for 10 minutes or until the flesh is cooked and the shell is a deep red colour. Transfer the crab to a bowl and set aside, then place the roasting tin over medium heat on the stovetop. Pour in the wine to deglaze and simmer until reduced by half.

Heat the remaining 20 ml olive oil in a heavy-based saucepan over medium heat, add the onion, capsicum, carrot, celery, fennel and finely chopped garlic and saute until soft and translucent. Add the tomato and cook to a paste, about 10 minutes. Add the chopped redfish and the reserved crab, then cook, stirring, until the fish has firmed up, about 10 minutes. Add the stock, then pour in enough water to cover (about 650 ml). Season with a pinch of salt and simmer gently for 45 minutes, skimming regularly.

While the bouillabaisse is simmering, make the rouille. Scoop out 100 ml of the simmering stock and place in a small saucepan over low heat. Add the saffron and fish liver, if using, and poach gently until the liver is just firm. Remove from the heat and take out the liver, then stir in the breadcrumbs and allow them to absorb the stock to make a paste.

≥

∨

ROUILLE

small pinch of saffron threads

20 g fish liver (optional)

1 tablespoon breadcrumbs, preferably sourdough

3 garlic cloves, peeled

salt flakes

2 egg yolks

squeeze of lemon juice

250 ml (1 cup) extra virgin olive oil, ideally something delicate and not too spicy

pinch of cayenne pepper

CROUTONS

1 baguette, cut into thin slices on the diagonal

olive oil, for brushing

Using a mortar and pestle, pound the garlic to a paste with a pinch of salt, then add the poached liver, if using, and pound again until smooth.

Separately pass the bread paste and the garlic paste through a fine-meshed sieve. If you're happy with a more rustic sauce, feel free to skip this step.

Whisk the egg yolks with the lemon juice and bread paste, then gradually whisk in the oil drop by drop to emulsify – the rouille should be the consistency of a thick mayonnaise. Slowly add the garlic paste until the desired flavour is reached. Adjust the seasoning with lemon juice and salt and add the cayenne pepper to give a light heat to the sauce.

Push the bouillabaisse through a mouli (if you don't have a mouli, press the soup through a colander with the back of a ladle), then strain through a muslin-lined sieve into a clean pan, discarding the solids. Don't be tempted to use a food processor or your soup will be chalky-textured from the pulverised fishbones.

About 30 minutes before you want to serve, preheat the oven to 200°C.

Bring a saucepan of salted water to the boil and simmer the potatoes until tender. Drain and peel, then cut into 1.5 cm thick slices.

For the croutons, brush the baguette slices with olive oil and toast in the oven for 15 minutes until golden and crisp.

Meanwhile, bring the pan of bouillabaisse to a simmer. Add the saffron and simmer for 5 minutes, then taste and adjust the seasoning with salt, pepper and lemon juice if necessary. Add the potato slices and the bruised garlic cloves and gently warm through for 3 minutes, taking care that the potato doesn't break up. Remove the garlic clove.

Wipe the garlic oil off the fish, then place in a baking dish, skin-side up. Pour over about 250 ml (1 cup) of the bouillabaisse, just to moisten, then cover with foil and bake for 5 minutes or until just cooked.

Divide the fish among shallow bowls, then pour over the bouillabaisse and potatoes and scatter over the reserved fennel fronds. Serve with a bowl of rouille and the toasted baguette slices on the side. If there's any spare bouillabaisse, place it in the middle of the table for top-ups.

OATCAKES WITH FARMHOUSE CHEDDAR & CHUTNEY

1 × 360 g wedge of farmhouse
 cheddar
chutney, ideally homemade pear
 & tomato (see page 220),
 to serve

OATCAKES
325 g rolled oats
pinch of fine salt
¼ teaspoon bicarbonate of soda
20 g beef fat or butter, melted
about 125 ml (½ cup) hot water

This is great as a cheese course or snack. For the oatcakes, ask your butcher for some beef fat (tallow) or keep the drippings from your Sunday roast. This recipe makes about 20 oatcakes, which can be stored in an airtight container for up to 2 weeks.

For the oatcakes, combine the oats, salt and bicarbonate of soda in a large bowl, then add the melted beef fat or butter and stir well. Pour in just enough hot water to form a firm dough – use your hands to bring the dough together. Roll into a large sausage about 5 cm in diameter and wrap in cling film while the dough is still warm, then chill in the fridge for an hour to firm.

Preheat the oven to 200°C and line a baking tray with baking paper.

Remove the dough from the fridge and cut into 5 mm thick slices, taking care to remove the plastic from the slices of dough, then place on the prepared tray. Bake the oatcakes for 10 minutes or until golden and firm. Cool on the baking tray for a few minutes then transfer to a wire rack to cool completely.

Place the wedge of cheddar on a platter with the oatcakes and a jar of chutney on the side.

RED RICE & WHITE QUINOA WITH BASIL & PEAS

SERVES 4–6

150 g Camargue red rice

150 g white quinoa

1 bunch spring onions, white parts only, thinly sliced

400 g fresh peas, shelled

1 bunch basil, leaves picked and torn

1 punnet pea tendrils or snowpea shoots, picked

BASIL OIL

1 bunch basil

250 ml (1 cup) grapeseed oil

pinch of salt flakes

Camargue red rice originated in the sixteenth century in the marshes of the region of the same name, in southern France. It has a firm texture, somewhere between brown and wild rice, with a delicious nutty flavour. There are three types of quinoa – white, red and black – the main difference being that the red and black grains tend to stay a little firmer when cooked and so hold their shape better. I've used white here for a greater contrast of colour and texture with the red rice, but you can choose any you like. Frozen peas or broad beans are fantastic to have on hand for those days when you don't have time to shell fresh ones, or they're out of season.

The leftover basil oil will keep for up to 3 months in a screwtop jar in the fridge, and is delicious on salads, especially ones with avocados or tomatoes, or drizzled over fish and vegetables.

For the basil oil, place the basil, oil and salt in a small saucepan and gently warm to 80°C. Blitz in an upright blender or powerful food processor for 2 minutes. (The faster the blades spin, the finer the basil will be chopped, and the more deeply coloured and flavoured your basil oil will be.) Strain the basil oil through a sieve lined with three layers of muslin, so you don't get any tiny specks of basil in the oil – these would eventually turn your oil brown.

Cook the rice in a saucepan of lightly salted water for 20 minutes, then drain thoroughly.

Meanwhile, cook the quinoa in a saucepan of lightly salted water for 14 minutes, then drain well.

Blanch the peas by plunging them into salted boiling water and simmering until just tender, then drain well.

Place the rice, quinoa, spring onion, peas and basil leaves in a bowl, add 2 tablespoons of the basil oil and gently toss together. Transfer to a platter. Garnish with the pea shoots and drizzle with another 2 tablespoons of basil oil, then serve.

GREEN BEANS, SNOWPEAS, HAZELNUTS, DRIED FIGS & FETA

SERVES 4

70 g hazelnuts

400 g green beans, topped and tailed

400 g snowpeas (mangetout), topped and tailed

200 g dried figs, cut into strips

1 bunch mint, leaves picked and torn

3 tablespoons extra virgin olive oil

1 tablespoon red wine vinegar

salt flakes and freshly ground black pepper

120 g Persian feta

handful of snowpea shoots, to serve

This is a version of one of my wife Joss's salads that I eat at home a lot. There are very few ingredients, so the salad relies heavily on good-quality produce. Any kind of feta will work here, but the lovely creamy texture of Persian feta gives you the option of scattering the cheese on top or tossing it through the salad to form a chunky dressing that coats the beans and figs.

Preheat the oven to 180°C. Scatter the hazelnuts on a baking tray and toast in the oven for 5 minutes or until golden. Let them cool, then remove the skins by rubbing the nuts in a clean tea towel. Give them a tap with a rolling pin to break but not crush them.

Blanch the beans and snowpeas separately in a saucepan of salted boiling water until just tender. Plunge into a bowl of iced water to stop the cooking process, then drain and spin in a salad spinner or pat dry with a clean tea towel.

Place the hazelnuts, beans, snowpeas, figs, mint, olive oil and vinegar in a bowl, season with salt and pepper and gently toss to combine. Taste and adjust the seasoning if necessary.

At this point you can either add half of the feta and toss lightly so the cheese combines with the dressing to become nice and creamy, then add the rest in blobs, or just put the salad on a serving platter and dollop all of the cheese on top. Drizzle over a little oil from the feta, garnish with snowpea shoots and serve.

YOUNG SPRING VEGETABLES WITH ANCHOIADE

SERVES 4

1 bunch green asparagus, bottoms snapped and stalks peeled if necessary

12 green beans, topped and tailed

12 young, tender broad beans

12 snowpeas (mangetout), topped and tailed

2 baby fennel bulbs, cut into quarters lengthways

3 celery hearts, cut into short lengths

12 baby carrots, ideally heirloom varieties

1 bunch radishes, leaves on

1 bunch spring onions

6 baby cucumbers

ANCHOIADE

1 garlic clove, chopped

1 hard-boiled egg, peeled and chopped

2 teaspoons salted capers, rinsed and patted dry

140 g anchovy fillets in oil, drained

small handful of savory, sage or tarragon leaves, finely chopped

finely grated zest and juice of ½ lemon

50 ml extra virgin olive oil

Use whatever seasonal young vegetables look good and fresh at the market for this celebration of springtime. An anchovy dip from Provence in France, anchoiade is perfect with a glass of rose to hand or just spread on toast. Essentially, it is a pimped-up gentleman's relish and is all about the anchovies. Buy the best you can afford – I always look for Ortiz, a Spanish brand stocked by most good food stores.

To make the anchoiade, place the garlic, egg and capers in a mortar and pestle and crush to a paste. Add the anchovies, savory and lemon zest and juice and grind together, then stir in the olive oil to form a coarse paste. (If you prefer, you can make this in a blender or food processor, but I think you get a much better texture with a mortar and pestle.) Transfer the anchoiade to a small serving bowl.

If the vegetables have just been harvested and are jumping out of their skins with freshness, leave them raw, as they will be very crisp and sweet. If not, blanch all the vegetables except the radishes, spring onions and cucumbers in a saucepan of salted boiling water until just tender.

Serve the vegetables on a platter with the anchoiade for dipping.

TREACLE-CURED OCEAN TROUT WITH SUGARSNAPS & MUSTARD VINAIGRETTE

SERVES 4

200 g sugarsnap peas

1 golden shallot, finely diced

large handful of watercress sprigs

handful of dill sprigs

rye bread, butter and lemon wedges, to serve

TREACLE-CURED OCEAN TROUT

40 g black treacle, warmed

1 teaspoon fennel seeds, toasted and lightly crushed

finely grated zest of ½ lemon

2 teaspoons mustard powder

2 tablespoons salt flakes

½ teaspoon freshly ground black pepper

1 × 400 g ocean trout fillet, skin on, trimmed and pin-boned

MUSTARD & VERJUS VINAIGRETTE

2 teaspoons Dijon mustard

1 teaspoon verjus

salt flakes and freshly ground white pepper

2 teaspoons vegetable oil

1 tablespoon extra virgin olive oil

This is such a simple recipe. It has become my go-to method of curing, and works just as well with duck breast or lean pieces of pork fillet as it does for oily fish.

It's worth making a double batch – about a whole side of fish – of this cured ocean trout, as it will keep for a minimum of a week in the fridge, and is hard to resist in a fresh sourdough roll with piccalilli (see page 220) and watercress, or as the starting point for a salad with beetroot and horseradish (see page 122).

To prepare the ocean trout, combine the treacle, fennel seeds, lemon zest, mustard powder, salt and pepper and spread evenly over the fish. Wrap in cling film and place on a tray, skin-side down. Leave in the fridge for 12 hours.

The next day, remove the cured ocean trout from the fridge and pat dry with paper towel, removing all the curing liquid. Place the ocean trout on a board and cut into thin slices.

Lightly blanch the sugarsnaps by plunging them into salted boiling water and simmering until just tender, then drain well. Place in a bowl, together with the shallot, watercress and dill.

For the vinaigrette, whisk the mustard and vinegar together with a pinch of salt and a grinding of white pepper, then slowly drizzle in the oils to emulsify into a thick vinaigrette.

Add the vinaigrette to the bowl with the sugarsnaps and gently toss, then serve alongside the fish.

Eat with thin slices of rye bread, generously buttered, and lemon wedges for squeezing.

JEFF'S LAZY SUSHI

SERVES 4

1 sheet nori

½ teaspoon harissa (see page 233) or chilli paste

½ bunch chives, snipped

1 punnet purple shiso cress, picked

handful of coriander leaves

1 pomelo or pink grapefruit, segmented

2 spring onions, sliced into rings

1 tablespoon ocean trout roe

12 slices pickled ginger

¼ teaspoon white sesame seeds, toasted

¼ teaspoon black sesame seeds

finely grated fresh wasabi or horseradish, to taste

KINGFISH SASHIMI

2 jalapeno chillies, chopped

10 g bonito flakes

½ teaspoon finely grated lime zest

1 tablespoon salt flakes

400 g sashimi-grade kingfish fillet, skin removed

SUSHI RICE

200 g (1 cup) sushi rice

30 ml Japanese rice vinegar

15 g caster sugar

GINGER & LIME DRESSING

2 tablespoons ginger vinegar

1 teaspoon lime juice

2 tablespoons soy sauce

2 tablespoons extra virgin olive oil

Jeffrey De Rome, a classically trained chef, has worked with me since 2007 – and over that time, I have been privileged to see him develop into an amazing chef. He now runs the kitchen at Kitchen by Mike, and we collaborate very closely. So when I wanted to serve some semi-cured kingfish I had prepared, Jeff took his inspiration from relaxed chirashi-style sushi to come up with this treat. The kingfish needs to marinate for 12 hours, so start well ahead of time. You can use other oily fish, such as tuna, salmon or ocean trout. If you can't find ginger vinegar (look for the Yamato brand), then use the syrup from a jar of pickled ginger.

Tempura crumbs add a nice crunch to the dish. To make them, mix 1 part plain flour and 2 parts iced water into a rough slurry. Scatter into a pan of hot oil and deep-fry the little scraps of batter until crisp. Remove with a slotted spoon and drain on paper towel, then scatter over the sushi before serving.

For the kingfish sashimi, blend together the chilli, bonito, zest and salt in a small food processor. Rub over the kingfish fillet, then wrap in cling film and marinate in the fridge for 12 hours.

For the sushi rice, rinse the rice until the water runs clear, then drain well. If you have a rice cooker, place the rice in the cooker with 310 ml (1¼ cups) cold water and cook for 15 minutes, then leave on the 'warm' setting for 10 minutes (don't lift the lid!). If you don't have a rice cooker, combine the rice and water in a heavy-based saucepan and bring to the boil. Cover and reduce the heat to its lowest setting, then cook very gently for 15 minutes. Remove from the heat and leave with the lid on to steam for 10 minutes.

Meanwhile, combine the vinegar and sugar in a small saucepan and simmer for 3 minutes. Gently fold this into the warm rice, then cover and keep warm until needed.

To make the ponzu dressing, strain the ginger vinegar through a fine-meshed sieve into a small bowl, then whisk in the lime juice, soy sauce and olive oil.

Toast the nori sheet by waving it gently over a gas burner or other open flame, keeping it about 20 cm away from the flame – it will shrink slightly when it is ready. If it starts to colour, it means it is burning and will taste bitter, so take your time and toast it very slowly. Allow to cool and tear into 2 cm pieces.

Scatter the rice over a large platter. Cut the marinated kingfish into 5 mm thick slices and arrange on the rice, then pour the ponzu dressing evenly over the fish. Smear the harissa or chilli paste on the side of the platter, so people can adjust the heat level of the dressing to their taste. Scatter the remaining ingredients over the top and serve.

32

HAM KNUCKLE & DUCK TERRINE WITH CORNICHONS & RADISHES

SERVES 10

2 × 1 kg unsmoked ham hocks

1 small onion, roughly chopped

1 small carrot, roughly chopped

small handful of parsley stalks

2 bay leaves

100 ml white wine vinegar

10 white peppercorns

salt flakes

1 tablespoon wholegrain mustard

handful of flat-leaf parsley leaves, finely chopped

freshly ground black pepper

15 thin slices serrano ham

90 g (½ cup) cornichons

2 bunches radishes, ideally French breakfast, leaves on

four-spice salt (see page 228), to serve

1 loaf sourdough bread, cut into 1 cm thick slices and toasted

DUCK CONFIT

6 duck legs (marylands)

3 teaspoons salt flakes

10 white peppercorns

10 garlic cloves, peeled

3 bay leaves

small handful of parsley stalks

6 thyme sprigs

125 ml (½ cup) white wine

about 1.2 kg duck fat, melted

This is the finest picnic food imaginable. As the duck needs to be salted the day before and the terrine needs to set overnight, you'll need to start the recipe a couple of days ahead. The finished terrine will keep for up to a week in the fridge – though it rarely lasts that long in our house, as it's so hard to resist with a slice of toast or baguette. To lift the terrine a notch for a special occasion, sandwich a ribbon of foie gras down the middle when filling the mould.

For the duck confit, sprinkle the duck legs with the salt and leave overnight.

The next day, preheat the oven to 120°C and line a baking dish with baking paper. Brush off the salt and wipe all moisture from the duck legs, then place them in the baking dish, skin-side down. Add the remaining ingredients, making sure there is enough duck fat to cover the legs. Cover tightly with baking paper and a double layer of foil, then cook gently in the oven for 4 hours or until the flesh falls from the bone.

Meanwhile, place the ham hocks in a stockpot or large saucepan with the onion, carrot, parsley stalks, bay leaves, white wine vinegar, peppercorns and 1 tablespoon of salt flakes. Pour in 2 litres of water, cover and simmer very gently, skimming regularly, for 3 hours or until the flesh starts to fall from the bone.

Remove the duck legs from the confit and the ham hocks from the pot. When they are both cool enough to handle but still warm, strip the meat from the bones. Gently massage a ladleful of the confit juices and fat into the shredded meat, adding more if needed to moisten. Take care not to over-mix or the texture will become too paste-like – you want to keep the large shards of meat intact. Mix in the mustard and chopped parsley, and season to taste with salt and pepper.

Line a 1.25 litre terrine mould with cling film, leaving an overhang all around. Fill with the meat mixture, then fold the overhanging cling film over the top of the meat, place a board on top and weigh down with a few tins of tomatoes or similar. Leave to set in the fridge overnight.

The next day, remove the terrine from the mould and take off the cling film. Carefully wrap the terrine with slices of serrano ham, then wrap tightly in cling film and return to the fridge until needed.

When you are ready to eat, cut the terrine into finger-width slices and serve with a pile of cornichons and radishes, a small bowl of four-spice salt and slices of toasted sourdough.

ROSEMARY & GARLIC FOCACCIA

SERVES 8

1 kg unbleached baker's flour,
  plus extra for dusting

1 teaspoon dried yeast

2 tablespoons salt flakes,
  plus extra for sprinkling

1 bunch rosemary, leaves picked

10 garlic cloves, thinly sliced

125 ml (½ cup) extra virgin
  olive oil

This focaccia is wonderful simply dunked in olive oil or served with dips. It's also great alongside a hearty soup, and makes delicious sandwiches: just split a slice in two and fill with rocket and prosciutto. For a change, turn it into olive bread by scattering the top with pitted olives and allowing the dough to prove and rise a little around the olives before baking, or scatter the top with caramelised onions and thyme.

Place the flour, yeast and 700 ml of water in the bowl of an electric mixer fitted with a dough hook and mix on low speed for 2 minutes. Cover and leave to rest for 30 minutes.

Add the salt to the dough and mix on high speed until it starts to come away from the side of the bowl and is smooth and no longer sticky, about 5 minutes. Tip the dough into a lightly oiled bowl, then cover and leave to prove in a warm place for about 1 hour or until doubled in size.

Lightly oil a large baking tray. Turn out the dough onto a lightly floured benchtop and form into a rectangle that will fit the baking tray. Transfer the dough to the tray and dimple with your fingers so the dough covers the whole tray. Cover and leave to rest in the fridge overnight.

The next day, the dough should have proved and doubled in size. Lightly dimple the dough again with your fingertips. Mix together the rosemary, garlic and olive oil and spread evenly over the dough, then sprinkle with a little extra salt. Leave at room temperature for 30 minutes.

Preheat the oven to 230°C.

Bake the focaccia for 20 minutes or until golden. Allow to cool slightly on the tray, then gently transfer to a board and cut into pieces to serve. This is best eaten on the day it's baked.

36 CRUSHED BROAD BEAN, GRILLED ASPARAGUS & PECORINO TARTINE

SERVES 4

4 thick slices sourdough bread

2 bunches green asparagus, bottoms snapped

60 ml (¼ cup) extra virgin olive oil, plus extra for drizzling

1 kg broad beans, podded

120 g pecorino, half grated and half shaved

pinch of salt flakes

2 garlic cloves, peeled and cut in half

handful of baby sorrel, young red chard or baby spinach leaves

freshly ground black pepper

Springtime on a plate! Grilling the bread and asparagus over coals adds a lovely smokiness, but if this isn't possible, a chargrill or griddle pan will suffice. As this is such a simple dish, the ingredients need to be singing with freshness. Make this when the broad beans and asparagus are tender and at their peak, which is generally earlier in spring, and use new-season olive oil.

Brush the bread slices and asparagus spears with half the olive oil.

Meanwhile, cook the broad beans in a saucepan of boiling salted water for 5 minutes or until tender. Drain and lightly crush with the grated pecorino, a pinch of salt and a little olive oil.

Grill the bread and asparagus on a chargrill pan or under a hot grill. When the bread is nicely toasted, rub with the cut side of the garlic cloves.

Spoon the broad bean mixture over the toast and arrange the asparagus spears on top. Scatter over the sorrel leaves and finish with the shaved pecorino, a grinding of pepper and a drizzle of olive oil.

BAKED SQUID WITH BRAISED BEANS & CHORIZO

SERVES 4

1 tablespoon extra virgin olive oil

150 g chorizo, peeled and cut into chunks

600 g baby squid, with tentacles, rinsed and patted dry

small handful of flat-leaf parsley leaves, roughly chopped

lemon wedges, to serve

BRAISED BEANS & CHORIZO

250 g dried cannellini beans

pinch of bicarbonate of soda

75 ml extra virgin olive oil

200 g chorizo, peeled and cut into chunks

1 onion, finely diced

2 garlic cloves, thinly sliced

125 g piquillo peppers, seeds removed, cut into strips

1 tablespoon thyme leaves

2 teaspoons smoked sweet paprika

250 ml (1 cup) white wine

750 ml (3 cups) chicken stock (see page 241)

large handful of baby sorrel or spinach leaves

I love the flavours of Spain, particularly the wonderful bean stews.

If you're lucky enough to find little bottleneck squid the size of your thumb, there's no need to clean them inside, as they won't yet have grown a cellophane-like quill nor be big enough to eat fish. All they'll need is a quick rinse to remove any sand and grit. If the squid are larger than this, ask your fishmonger to clean them for you, keeping the tentacles. Piquillo peppers are available in jars at good delis, but at a pinch you could just use grilled capsicum to add a similar smoky-sweet flavour. Sorrel can be found at most farmers' markets – if you have no luck, a handful of baby spinach leaves is a great substitute. Don't forget to soak the cannellini beans the night before . . .

For the braised beans, soak the beans overnight in 1 litre (4 cups) of water with the bicarbonate of soda.

The next day, drain the beans and rinse well, then place in a saucepan, cover with fresh water and bring to the boil. Reduce the heat and simmer for 10 minutes, then drain and rinse again.

Heat the olive oil in a large ovenproof frying pan over medium heat, add the chorizo, onion and garlic and cook until the chorizo is golden brown and the onion and garlic are translucent. Add the piquillo pepper, thyme and paprika and saute for 5 minutes to lightly caramelise. Add the beans and wine and simmer until the liquid has reduced to a glaze. Add the stock and simmer very slowly for a further 2 hours or until the beans are tender. Scatter over the sorrel or spinach leaves and keep warm.

When the beans are almost ready, preheat the oven to 250°C.

Heat the olive oil in another frying pan over very high heat. Add the chorizo and saute until lightly caramelised, then add the squid and toss quickly. It is crucial that the pan is really, really hot, otherwise the squid will stew.

Tip the squid and chorizo into the pan of braised beans, then transfer to the oven and bake for 5–10 minutes or until the squid is tender and golden. Scatter over the chopped parsley and serve with lemon wedges.

40

OLD-SCHOOL FISH CAKES

SERVES 4

150 g hot-smoked kingfish fillet, skin and pinbones removed

150 g ocean trout fillet, skin and pinbones removed

150 g snapper fillet, skin and pinbones removed

750 ml (3 cups) full-cream milk

450 g sebago potatoes, peeled and cut into chunks

2 teaspoons mustard powder

1 small onion, finely diced

3 spring onions, thinly sliced

¼ bunch dill, leaves picked and roughly chopped

¼ bunch flat-leaf parsley, leaves picked and roughly chopped

salt flakes and freshly ground white pepper

150 g (1 cup) plain flour

4 eggs

140 g (2 cups) fresh breadcrumbs, ideally sourdough

4 tablespoons clarified butter or 2 tablespoons butter and 2 tablespoons olive oil

lemon wedges and tartare sauce (see page 240), to serve

I love fish cakes. They are such a great way to use up leftovers. For depth of flavour I like to include a third hot-smoked fish, like trout or kingfish, but the other two-thirds can be any other fish you choose – an oily fish such as ocean trout or salmon helps to keep the fish cakes moist. Tartare sauce and a squeeze of lemon is all these need, but for a more composed offering, serve with spinach and a pool of parsley sauce (see page 236).

Place the fish fillets in a saucepan with 500 ml (2 cups) of the milk and poach gently for about 5 minutes or until just cooked. Remove from the heat and leave the fish to cool slightly in the poaching liquid, then drain.

Boil the potatoes until tender, then drain and mash until smooth. While still hot, mix with the fish, mustard powder, onion, spring onion and chopped herbs and season to taste with salt and pepper. Try to keep the fish in nice flakes for texture, and don't over-work it with the potato or it will be like eating hairy mashed potato! Press the mixture into a baking dish to form a 3 cm thick layer and chill in the fridge for at least 1 hour to firm.

Cut the chilled fish cake mixture into four patties using a large round cutter. Season the flour with salt and place in a shallow bowl. Whisk the eggs with the remaining 250 ml (1 cup) of milk and place in another shallow bowl. Tip the breadcrumbs into a third bowl. Gently toss the fish cakes in the flour to give an even dusting, then dunk them in the egg mixture until completely coated. Finally, press them into the breadcrumbs, reshaping them neatly with a palette knife as you go.

Heat the clarified butter or butter and oil in a large frying pan over medium heat and cook the fish cakes until they are golden brown and crisp on both sides and warmed through. Take care to keep the crumbs in place as you turn them. Remove and drain on paper towel.

Serve with lemon wedges and a small bowl of tartare sauce on the side.

BEER-CAN ROAST JERK CHICKEN WITH LIME & CORIANDER

SERVES 4

1 × 1.8 kg chicken
1 × 375 ml can beer
lime wedges and coriander leaves,
  to serve

JERK CHICKEN MARINADE

½ teaspoon ground cloves
1 teaspoon freshly ground
  black pepper
4 teaspoons ground allspice
1 teaspoon ground coriander
½ teaspoon freshly grated nutmeg
1 teaspoon ground cinnamon
1 tablespoon thyme leaves
10 garlic cloves, roughly chopped
½ bunch coriander, washed and
  roughly chopped (leaves, stems
  and roots)
2 spring onions, roughly chopped
1–2 long red chillies, roughly
  chopped
2 cm knob ginger, roughly chopped
1 tablespoon muscovado sugar
  or brown sugar
finely grated zest and juice of
  1 large or 2 small limes
pinch of salt flakes
125 ml (½ cup) vegetable oil

My time in London, especially in Brixton and at the Notting Hill Carnival, inspired this popular dish. Jerk is taken very seriously by the Jamaican community, and everyone has their own handed-down spice blend, but allspice is always in the mix. We luxed our version by roasting the marinated chicken over a beer can. Not only does this enable the heat to circulate all around the bird, but the steam generated from the half-full can of beer also helps to keep the meat moist. You can use any canned beer, but for an authentically Jamaican result, Red Stripe is the only way to go.

This is delicious served with the corn on page 81 or the red rice & quinoa with basil & peas on page 23.

To make the jerk chicken marinade, blend all the ingredients to paste in a food processor.

Truss the chicken to help it cook evenly. Stir half the beer into the marinade and rub all over the chicken (save the rest of the beer – and the can – for later), then leave to marinate overnight in the fridge.

The next day, preheat the oven to 220°C. Place the half-full beer can in the middle of a roasting tin, then carefully up-end the chicken over the can, so the chicken stands upright. Roast the chicken for 25 minutes, then reduce the temperature to 180°C and cook for a further 20 minutes. Turn off the oven and prop the door ajar, then leave the chicken to rest in the oven for 15 minutes.

Joint the chicken, then serve with lime wedges and a good scattering of coriander leaves.

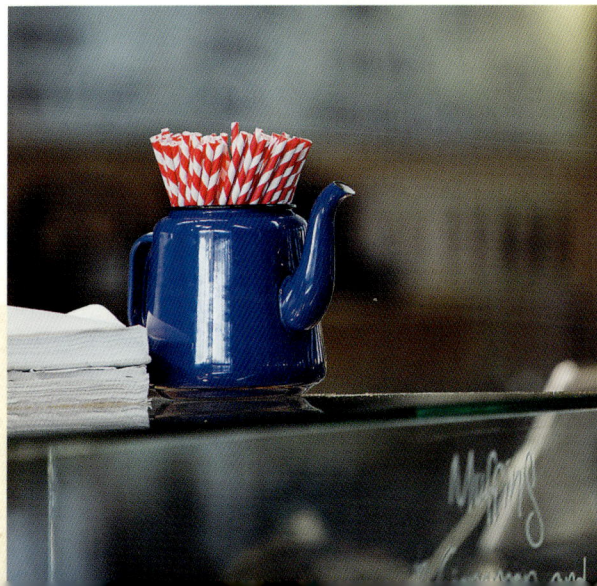

44

POT-ROAST DUCK WITH BRAISED PEAS & LETTUCE

SERVES 4

1 × 2.1 kg duck
salt flakes
2 tablespoons olive oil
120 g bacon, cut into lardons
12 golden shallots, peeled
12 garlic cloves, peeled
1 tablespoon thyme leaves
2 bay leaves
80 ml (⅓ cup) white wine

BRAISED PEAS & LETTUCE

20 g butter
100 g bacon, cut into lardons
8 golden shallots, peeled
1 teaspoon plain flour
about 200 ml chicken stock
  (see page 241), warmed
500 g canned or frozen baby peas
pinch of caster sugar
pinch of salt flakes
pinch of freshly ground
  white pepper
1 baby cos lettuce, finely shredded

This is the perfect spring meal for four people.

Ask your butcher to truss the duck for you, so it will cook evenly. Start the braised peas about half an hour before you want to eat – the vegetables need to be served promptly after cooking, or the lettuce will start to go brown. You can of course use fresh or frozen peas in this recipe; however, it's worth making an effort to find the tiny sweet canned peas in a sweet-salty liquor that are a prized possession in the French larder. The brand to look for is D'aucy – and trust me, once you try them, you will be hooked. I love them on toast with a fried egg and anchovies.

Preheat the oven to 100°C.

Season the duck with salt. Heat the olive oil in a deep flameproof casserole dish with a lid over medium–high heat and sear the bird all over to give it a nice deep golden brown colour. Remove the duck and set aside, then add the bacon and shallots and saute until golden.

Return the duck to the casserole dish, along with the garlic, thyme, bay leaves and wine, then cover with the lid and roast in the oven for 3 hours. Remove from the oven and allow to rest for 15 minutes before carving.

About 15 minutes before the duck is due to come out of the oven, start the braised peas and lettuce. Melt half the butter in a frying pan over medium heat. Add the bacon and shallots and saute until golden, then remove from the pan. Add the flour and stir for 2 minutes, then add a quarter of the stock and stir until smooth. Simmer for 1 minute, then add the bacon, shallots, peas, sugar, salt and pepper. Stir well, then add just enough stock to come to the level of the peas, cover with a round of baking paper and simmer for 20 minutes. Remove the pan from the heat and, just before serving, stir in the shredded lettuce and remaining butter to give a nice glaze.

Strain the juice from the pot-roast duck into a gravy boat or tip it over the peas. Carve the duck breast from the bone and arrange on plates with the legs. Serve with the braised peas and lettuce on the side.

LAMB SHOULDER WITH WHITE BEANS

SERVES 8

125 g dried cannellini beans

pinch of bicarbonate of soda

15 g duck fat or 15 ml olive oil

1 × 2 kg lamb shoulder, on the bone

450 g pork belly, skin on, cut into strips

1 small onion, diced

1 large carrot, diced

½ small swede, diced

1 small leek, cut into quarters lengthways then sliced

200 ml white wine

about 1 litre chicken stock (see page 241)

1 bay leaf

200 g kale, well washed, stems chopped and leaves shredded

350 g waxy potatoes (such as nicola), diced

handful of flat-leaf parsley leaves, chopped

handful of marjoram leaves, chopped

5 garlic cloves, crushed

salt flakes and freshly ground white pepper

8 thick slices sourdough bread

150 ml extra virgin olive oil

Lamb in spring is a wonderful thing. This is a light and soupy dish that can be left in a low oven while you get on with your day. If you want to use leg instead of shoulder, try using hogget or mutton as the fat content is important to keep the meat moist during the long, slow cooking. A large flameproof casserole or heavy-based roasting tin that can go from the stovetop to the oven is ideal here. Because the beans need that all-important overnight soak, you'll need to start the day before.

Soak the beans overnight in 1 litre (4 cups) of water with the bicarbonate of soda.

The next day, drain the beans and rinse well, then place in a saucepan, cover with fresh water and bring to the boil. Reduce the heat and simmer for 10 minutes, then drain and rinse again.

Heat the duck fat or olive oil in a large flameproof casserole or heavy-based roasting tin over medium–high heat and sear the lamb shoulder on all sides until well coloured. Remove the lamb, then add the pork, onion, carrot, swede and leek and saute until lightly coloured. Add the wine and simmer until reduced by half.

Return the lamb, along with the beans, and pour in enough stock to cover the beans by about 2 cm. Add the bay leaf, then cover with baking paper and simmer gently for 2 hours or until the beans are tender and the meat is falling off the bone. Alternatively, cook in a preheated 130°C oven for the same amount of time. Check the liquid levels regularly and top up with more stock as needed.

When the lamb and beans are done, add the kale, potato and parsley and cook for another 30 minutes or until the potato is just cooked. Add the marjoram and garlic, then taste and adjust the seasoning if necessary. Take off the heat and leave to stand for 20 minutes, then remove the lamb, tear off the meat in large hunks and return it to the casserole or tin.

To serve, put a slice of bread in the base of each bowl and douse generously with olive oil. Ladle the lamb, beans and vegetables over the top.

GLUTEN-FREE LEMON MERINGUE PIE

MAKES 1 LARGE PIE OR 6 SMALL ONES

250 g lemon curd (see page 219)
pure icing sugar, for dusting

MERINGUE

120 g caster sugar
2 egg whites

GLUTEN-FREE SWEET PASTRY

150 g rice flour, plus extra
    for dusting
150 g chickpea flour
1 teaspoon xanthan gum
100 g ground almonds
100 g pure icing sugar
160 g chilled unsalted butter,
    diced
2 eggs

This is a great recipe to use up any leftover lemon curd and egg whites. It's also a handy one to have in your repertoire of gluten-free treats. Xanthan gum is available from health-food stores and some supermarkets, as are rice flour and chickpea flour (the latter is sometimes labelled besan or gram flour).

The amount of pastry here is the smallest amount that can be successfully made in a food processor, but the leftover dough can be frozen for several months.

For the pastry, sift the dry ingredients into the bowl of a food processor. Add the butter bit by bit, pulsing it into the flour until the mixture resembles breadcrumbs. Add the eggs one at a time and pulse until a smooth dough forms.

Remove the dough from the food processor and roll into two balls. Slightly flatten each ball with a rolling pin to make a 2 cm thick disc. Wrap the discs in cling film and place one in the freezer and the other in the fridge to rest for 30 minutes.

Preheat the oven to 190°C. Lightly dust your bench with rice flour. Roll out the disc of chilled dough to a 2 mm thickness and use to line one large (about 26 cm) round tart tin or six small tart tins. Prick the pastry all over with a fork and place a sheet of baking paper on top, then fill with pastry weights, dried beans or rice.

Place the tart shells in the oven and blind bake for 15 minutes to set the dough. Remove the paper and weights and bake for another 10 minutes or until the pastry is golden and dry. Allow to cool on a wire rack.

Meanwhile, for the meringue, increase the oven temperature to 200°C. Line a baking tray with baking paper, then scatter over the sugar and warm it in the oven until the edges are just melting, about 3 minutes – keep a close eye on it, so you don't end up with caramel.

Whisk the egg whites in an electric mixer until soft peaks form. Add the warmed sugar and mix on the highest speed for 5 minutes until the mixture is very stiff and glossy and the sugar has completely dissolved.

When the pastry has cooled, fill with cold lemon curd. Using a piping bag or spatula, pile a healthy amount of meringue on top of the curd. Place under a very hot grill or blast with a kitchen blowtorch until the meringue is firm and lightly caramelised. Chill in the fridge for 15 minutes to firm slightly, then dust with icing sugar and serve.

RHUBARB CRUMBLE

RHUBARB CRUMBLE CAKE

MAKES 1 × 26 CM CAKE

2 bunches rhubarb, trimmed,
  washed and cut into 5 cm
  lengths
100 g caster sugar
500 g plain flour
1 teaspoon baking powder
250 g chilled unsalted butter,
  diced
2 tablespoons desiccated coconut
pure icing sugar, for dusting
creme fraiche or chantilly cream
  (see page 55), to serve

What do you call a cross between a tart and cake? A take . . . This is such an interesting recipe, with a pastry-like base and a cake-like filling, both made from the same mixture. The dough is compressed to make the base, then the remaining dough is lightly crumbled into the centre. You can use any poached or baked fruit in the filling, or try using jam – too easy!

Preheat the oven to 180°C and grease a 26 cm springform tin.

Toss the rhubarb and sugar together in a bowl. Transfer to a baking dish, then cover with foil and bake for about 20 minutes until tender, shaking the dish occasionally so the rhubarb cooks evenly. Resist the temptation to stir, or the stems will lose their shape and disintegrate. Remove from the oven and leave to cool.

Meanwhile, sift the flour and baking powder into the bowl of a food processor and add the butter bit by bit, pulsing it into the flour until the mixture resembles breadcrumbs. Set aside 500 g of the crumbs for the filling.

Gather the rest of the crumbs together and use your hands to form into a ball. Slightly flatten with a rolling pin to make a 2 cm thick disc. Wrap in cling film and leave to rest for 30 minutes at room temperature.

Unwrap the dough and press into the prepared tin with your fingers, easing it into the base and up the sides. Scatter in half of the reserved crumbs, then spread with the rhubarb, reserving about 125 ml (½ cup) of the juices. Sprinkle in the remaining crumbs, then drizzle with the reserved rhubarb juices and scatter over the desiccated coconut.

Bake for 45 minutes or until golden and crisp, then leave to cool to room temperature so the cake firms up a little before you attempt to cut it.

Dust with icing sugar and serve with a bowl of creme fraiche or chantilly cream.

JAMMY DODGERS

MAKES ABOUT 12

125 g chilled butter, diced

55 g (⅓ cup) pure icing sugar, plus extra for dusting

pinch of salt flakes

½ teaspoon vanilla extract

110 g (¾ cup) plain flour

50 g (⅓ cup) cornflour

40 g (⅓ cup) ground hazelnuts

120 g raspberry jam, preferably homemade (see page 225)

These biscuits are my version of a playground favourite. They are very short and are delicious made with any jam. You can replace the ground hazelnuts with ground almonds, walnuts or pecans, if preferred. And you can make the biscuits as big or small as you like: for morning and afternoon tea, larger ones would be good, but smaller ones about 2 cm across are lovely as a bite with coffee.

Cream the butter, icing sugar and salt in an electric mixer for 5 minutes or until light and fluffy. Add the vanilla extract and mix until incorporated. Remove the bowl from the mixer and, using a metal spoon, fold in the flours and then the ground hazelnuts.

Use your hands to bring the dough together, then shape into a log about 5 cm in diameter. Wrap in cling film and leave to rest in the fridge for 1 hour.

Preheat the oven to 170°C and line a baking tray with baking paper.

Remove the dough from the fridge and cut into 5 mm-thick discs – you should get about 12 in all. Place the discs on the prepared tray and bake for 5 minutes, then open the oven door and carefully press the bowl of a teaspoon into the centre of each biscuit to make a cavity. Close the oven door and bake for a further 10–15 minutes or until golden. Cool on the tray for a few minutes, then transfer to a wire rack to cool completely.

While the biscuits are cooling, place the jam in a small saucepan over medium heat and simmer for a minute or two, so it will set more firmly in the biscuits. Spoon the jam evenly into the biscuit cavities and allow to cool and set. Dust with icing sugar just before serving.

BITTER CHOCOLATE TART

SERVES 12

3 eggs
3 egg yolks
60 g pure icing sugar
300 g butter
450 g dark chocolate (80% cocoa), broken into pieces
60 g natural cocoa powder
creme fraiche, to serve

CHOCOLATE PASTRY

350 g plain flour
40 g natural cocoa powder
125 g pure icing sugar
200 g cold butter, diced
finely grated zest of 1 orange
1 egg, lightly beaten

To make dutched (or dutch-processed) cocoa powder, the cocoa beans are washed with a potassium solution before being roasted and ground to produce a cocoa powder with a neutral acidity, while natural bitter cocoa is simply roasted beans pulverised to a fine powder. The natural bitter cocoa is best for this recipe, as its acidity will add another dimension of flavour, moderating the sweetness levels so you can serve the tart with creme fraiche without it being too cloying.

To make the chocolate pastry, combine the flour, cocoa powder and icing sugar in a bowl. Rub in the butter and orange zest with your fingertips until the mixture resembles fine breadcrumbs, then add the egg and gently mix to form a dough. (You could also do this in a food processor, if preferred.) Gather the dough into a ball, then wrap in cling film and leave to rest in the fridge for 1 hour.

Preheat the oven to 180°C. Roll out the pastry to a thickness of 2 mm and use to carefully line a 26 cm tart tin with a removable base. Prick the pastry all over with a fork and line with baking paper and pastry weights or dried beans, then blind-bake for 15 minutes. Remove the baking paper and weights or beans and return the tart shell to the oven for another 2 minutes to dry and crisp. Remove and set aside to cool, then turn the oven down to 150°C.

Place the eggs, egg yolks and icing sugar in the bowl of an electric mixer and whisk at high speed for 5 minutes or until the whisk leaves a figure-8 pattern when raised out of the mixture.

Heat the butter in a saucepan until melted and starting to bubble, then remove from the heat. Add the chocolate and cocoa powder and stir until melted and smooth – don't be tempted to speed this up by placing the pan back on the heat or the mixture will split.

Gently fold the chocolate mixture into the egg mixture, then pour into the tart shell. Bake the tart for 10 minutes or until the top is just set. Remove from the oven and leave to cool, then transfer to the fridge to firm for about an hour.

Bring to room temperature before cutting into thin wedges and serving with a dollop of creme fraiche.

MULBERRY MESS

SERVES 4

5 punnets mulberries
100 g pure icing sugar

MERINGUES
2 egg whites
120 g caster sugar

PISTACHIO BRITTLE
140 g (1 cup) unsalted pistachios
165 g (¾ cup) caster sugar
2 tablespoons golden syrup
30 g butter
¼ teaspoon bicarbonate of soda
pinch of salt flakes

CHANTILLY CREAM
600 ml whipping cream
60 g pure icing sugar
1 vanilla bean, split and
    seeds scraped

This is a twist on the classic strawberry, meringue and cream dessert of Eton Mess. This version reminds me of climbing mulberry trees as a child and getting in trouble for returning home with stained clothes. The meringues and the pistachio brittle can both be made ahead of time – then you're ready when the urge for a mess next strikes!

To make the meringues, preheat the oven to 200°C. Line a baking tray with baking paper, then scatter over the sugar and warm it in the oven until the edges are just melting, about 3 minutes – keep a close eye on it, so you don't end up with caramel. Whisk the egg whites in an electric mixer until soft peaks form. Add the warmed sugar and mix on the highest speed for 5 minutes until the mixture is very stiff and glossy and the sugar has completely dissolved.

Reduce the oven temperature to its lowest setting and line a baking tray with baking paper. Spoon the meringue onto the prepared tray in four mounds and bake for 6 hours or until crisp. (Keep an eye on the meringues and if they start to colour, turn off the oven and let them finish cooking in the residual heat.) Leave the meringues to cool in the switched-off oven. Remove when completely cold and store in an airtight container for up to a week.

To make the pistachio brittle, preheat the oven to 180°C. Scatter the pistachios on a baking tray and toast until golden and aromatic, about 8–10 minutes. Leave to cool. Line another baking tray with baking paper and place on a wire rack. Combine the sugar, golden syrup, butter and 2 tablespoons of hot water in a heavy-based saucepan and stir over medium heat until the sugar has dissolved. Simmer until the mixture is golden brown, then remove the pan from the heat and whisk in the bicarbonate of soda, salt and pistachios. Quickly pour onto the prepared tray, tilting the tray to spread it out – wear oven gloves to protect your hands from the molten praline. Leave to cool until rock-hard, then break into pieces and store in an airtight container for up to a week.

Blend 3 punnets of the mulberries with the icing sugar in a blender or just mix together, then pass through a fine-meshed sieve to remove the seeds and make a mulberry coulis.

To make the chantilly cream, whip the cream, icing sugar and vanilla seeds until soft peaks form.

When you're almost ready to serve, fold three-quarters of the mulberry coulis through the chantilly cream. Roughly break the meringues and layer one third in the base of a large dish or divide among four individual bowls, followed by half of the berry cream, another third of the meringue and the rest of the berry cream. Spoon over the remaining mulberry coulis and top with the rest of the mulberries, then scatter over the remaining meringue. Serve straightaway, garnished with a wedge of pistachio brittle.

56

BLOOD ORANGE CREME CARAMEL

SERVES 6

750 ml (3 cups) milk

finely grated zest of
   2 blood oranges

2 vanilla beans, split and
   seeds scraped

3 eggs

6 egg yolks

165 g caster sugar

CARAMEL

220 g (1 cup) caster sugar

1 vanilla bean, split and
   seeds scraped

Creme caramel is the simplest of desserts. The addition of blood orange zest gives a tangy twist to the classic combination of vanilla cream and slightly bitter caramel. (You only need the zest of the blood oranges for this recipe, but you can use the juice in the blood orange & Campari clutch start on page 12.) Don't be afraid to take the caramel to a deep crimson colour, as this will be what makes your creme caramel stand out from the pale, jelly-like imitators you see all too often!

To make the caramel, combine the sugar, scraped vanilla seeds and 2 tablespoons water in a small saucepan. Stir over low–medium heat until the sugar has dissolved, then bring to the boil and cook, without stirring, until the caramel is a deep crimson colour. Pour the caramel into a 20 cm round cake tin or six 200 ml heatproof moulds and leave to set for 30 minutes at room temperature.

Meanwhile, combine the milk, blood orange zest and vanilla seeds and bean in a saucepan and bring to a simmer. Remove from the heat and leave to infuse for 20 minutes.

Preheat the oven to 150°C.

Whisk the eggs, egg yolks and sugar in an electric mixer until the sugar has completely dissolved and the mixture is foamy. Whisk in the infused milk, then strain through a fine-meshed sieve and pour into the tin or moulds.

Place a cloth in the bottom of a large baking dish, then place the tin or moulds on top and pour enough hot water into the dish to come three-quarters of the way up the sides of the tin or moulds. Cook in the oven until the custard is just set but still has a slight wobble in the centre – about 15 minutes for individual creme caramels, 30–45 minutes for one large one.

Remove from the baking dish and leave to cool to room temperature. At this point, the creme caramel can be refrigerated for up to 3 days or served straightaway. I think it's best after a day in the fridge, as the moisture helps to release more of the caramel sauce.

To serve, dip the base of the tin or mould in boiling water for 5 seconds, then run a knife around the edge. Position a serving plate on top and carefully invert the creme caramel onto the plate.

SUM

CHAPTER

MER

2

CUCUMBER, MIRIN & SESAME SALAD

SERVES 4

2 long cucumbers
2 teaspoons black sesame seeds
2 teaspoons white sesame seeds
1 long red chilli, finely sliced
1 tablespoon toasted sesame oil
pinch of salt flakes
½ bunch coriander, sprigs picked

MIRIN & GINGER DRESSING

110 ml mirin
2 tablespoons Japanese
    rice vinegar
3 teaspoons soy sauce
3 cm knob ginger, finely chopped
2 red shallots, finely chopped

Black sesame seeds are available from Asian supermarkets and specialist spice suppliers, but if you can't find them, just use more of the white ones. As this dressing keeps well and is good with any green salad or steamed vegetables, or even an oyster, it's well worth making a double batch. Store the extra dressing in a screw-top jar in the fridge for up to 2 weeks.

For the dressing, mix all the ingredients together and leave to sit for a minimum of 1 hour before using.

Halve the cucumbers lengthways and use a teaspoon to scrape out the seeds, then cut on an angle into lengths about 10 cm × 1 cm. Place the cucumber in a large bowl.

Lightly toast the sesame seeds in a dry, heavy-based frying pan. Add to the bowl, along with the remaining ingredients. Pour over the dressing, toss everything together well and serve.

68

PEACH, RADICCHIO & FENNEL SALAD

SERVES 4

1 tablespoon raisins

1 teaspoon black tea leaves

handful of wild rocket

½ radicchio, leaves separated and torn into bite-size pieces

1 fennel bulb, finely sliced, fronds reserved

4 peaches, stones removed, cut into wedges

1 tablespoon pine nuts

ORANGE BLOSSOM DRESSING

30 ml orange blossom water

2 teaspoons honey

15 ml chardonnay vinegar

45 ml extra virgin olive oil

1 teaspoon thyme leaves

salt flakes and freshly ground black pepper, to taste

You can use white-flesh peaches or nectarines instead if you like. The only prerequisite is that the fruit is ripe and ready to eat, and so will be intense in flavour. Keep an eye out for stonefruit from Forbes, in New South Wales – I believe it is the very best you will ever taste. If peaches are out of season, try this with slices of crisp pear.

The recipe below makes 100 ml dressing, but the leftover dressing will keep for a week in the fridge and adds a lovely fresh, floral note to any green salad.

Place the raisins in a small bowl, cover with freshly brewed black tea and leave to plump for 30 minutes.

Meanwhile, to make the dressing, combine all the ingredients in a small jar or bottle and shake really hard to bring everything together.

In a large bowl, gently toss the rocket, radicchio, fennel and peach with 50 ml of the dressing. Arrange on a plate or platter, scatter with the drained raisins and the pine nuts, then drizzle with a tablespoon more of the dressing. Finish with the fennel fronds.

FIG, BLACK LENTIL, TREVISO & GOAT'S CHEESE SALAD

SERVES 4

1 red onion, very thinly sliced

2 tablespoons balsamic vinegar

salt flakes

100 g small black or puy-style lentils, soaked overnight

80 ml (⅓ cup) extra virgin olive oil

freshly ground black pepper

1 treviso radicchio, leaves separated and torn into bite-sized pieces

6 figs

60 g goat's cheese

handful of mint leaves

The best lentils to use for this salad are baby black lentils or green puy-style ones. I like to soak them overnight before steaming them – this method cooks the lentils perfectly while keeping them loose and light. Once you've cooked lentils this way, you won't go back!

If your figs are not perfectly ripe, drizzle them with a little balsamic vinegar and olive oil and roast them in a 180°C oven for 5 minutes to soften them and bring out their sweetness.

Mix the onion with the balsamic vinegar and a pinch of salt in a non-reactive bowl and allow to cure for 1 hour.

Meanwhile, drain the lentils, then place in a steamer and cook over boiling water for about 25 minutes until tender. If you don't have a steamer, cook the lentils in a saucepan of barely simmering water for about 15 minutes until just done. Drain the lentils and tip into a large bowl. Fork through a pinch of salt and half of the olive oil, then cover with cling film so the lentils stay moist.

When the onion is ready, mix it and the vinegar into the lentils and season with salt and pepper. Add the treviso and toss gently, then transfer to a platter. Cut the figs into wedges and place on top. Crumble over the goat's cheese and scatter with the mint. Finish with a few grindings of black pepper and drizzle with the remaining olive oil.

WATERMELON, MINT & TOMATO SALAD WITH CHILLI SALT

SERVES 4

¼ watermelon

320 g tomatoes, ideally heirloom varieties

handful of mint leaves

handful of basil leaves

2 tablespoons extra virgin olive oil

juice of 1 lemon

CHILLI SALT

6 dried long red chillies

6 teaspoons salt flakes

Nothing says summer like watermelon and tomato, and together they make a beautifully simple salad. Rather than wasting the watermelon rind, try pickling it using the same method as for cucumber pickle (see page 218); pickled watermelon rind goes perfectly with charcuterie.

This recipe makes more chilli salt than you need here, but it will keep in airtight jar for several months. Use it in my spicy version of a Bloody Mary (see page 62) or sprinkle it over some grilled sweetcorn.

First make the chilli salt. Preheat the grill to low. Place the chillies on the grill pan and toast under the grill for about 2 minutes until dark red.

Pulse the chilli in a spice grinder, or pound using a mortar and pestle, to form flakes. Add the salt and pulse or pound once or twice. You can make the chilli salt as coarse or fine as you wish – just blend longer for a finer finish.

Peel the melon, then cut the flesh into 5 cm chunks. Core the tomatoes then cut into wedges. Place the melon and tomato in a bowl, together with the mint and basil leaves and a pinch of chilli salt. Dress with olive oil and lemon juice to taste, gently tossing everything together.

Serve on a platter with more chilli salt on the side.

AVOCADO WITH BLACK BEAN VINAIGRETTE

SERVES 4–6

3 avocados

3 spring onions, cut into fine julienne strips

handful of coriander sprigs

1 tablespoon white sesame seeds, lightly toasted

1 tablespoon black sesame seeds

BLACK BEAN VINAIGRETTE

250 ml (1 cup) olive oil

90 g salted black beans

3 cm knob ginger, cut into fine julienne strips

3 garlic cloves, thinly sliced

1 small red capsicum (pepper), seeds and membrane removed, cut into 5 mm dice

100 ml Japanese rice vinegar

75 ml light soy sauce

about 2 teaspoons caster sugar

3 spring onions, thinly sliced

This has become a Kitchen by Mike classic. Given the choice, I prefer hass avocados, with their knobbly, brownish-black skin and creamy flesh, but the sleeker green shepard variety is also fine for this.

This recipe makes about 500 ml vinaigrettte, which is more than is needed here, but if you bottle the excess in sterilised jars (see page 224), it will keep for at least 3 months in your larder and is great served with raw seafood, barbecued meats or tossed through a stir-fry. Once opened, store in the fridge and use within 3 weeks.

To make the black bean vinaigrette, heat half of the olive oil in a small frying pan over low heat. Add the black beans and saute until the oil turns red and the beans become aromatic. Add the ginger, garlic and capsicum and saute until the capsicum is tender. Pour in the vinegar and soy sauce and bring to the boil. Taste to check the seasoning and adjust with sugar as necessary. Remove from the heat, then stir in the spring onion and the remaining olive oil. Allow to cool before using.

Cut the avocados in half and remove the seeds. Cut each avocado half in half again and arrange on a platter. Spoon vinaigrette into the cavity of each avocado quarter until full, then garnish with the spring onion and coriander. Scatter with the sesame seeds and serve.

Eat by holding an avocado quarter in the palm of your hand and scooping out the flesh and vinaigrette with a spoon. Messy, but worth it!

ROAST PUMPKIN WITH POMEGRANATE & NIGELLA SEEDS

SERVES 4

½ jap pumpkin (about 1.5 kg)
canola oil spray
salt flakes
1 tablespoon pomegranate seeds
1 tablespoon nigella seeds
handful of flat-leaf parsley leaves

POMEGRANATE MOLASSES DRESSING

75 ml pomegranate molasses
25 ml lime juice
150 ml extra virgin olive oil
salt flakes and freshly ground
   black pepper

This is a firm favourite at Kitchen by Mike – so much so that we daren't take it off the menu!

Preheat the oven to 220°C.

Cut the pumpkin into wedges, leaving the skin on. Place the wedges, skin side down, on a baking tray, spray with canola oil to coat evenly and sprinkle with salt.

Roast the pumpkin wedges for 30–45 minutes or until they are very soft with slightly burnt tips.

Meanwhile, for the dressing, whisk together the pomegranate molasses, lime juice and olive oil, then season to taste with salt and pepper.

Transfer the roast pumpkin to a bowl and pour over the dressing. Toss gently, then scatter with the pomegranate and nigella seeds and parsley.

Serve warm or at room temperature.

ROASTED RED CAPSICUMS WITH MOZZARELLA

SERVES 4

4 long red capsicums
  (bullhorn peppers)

1 tablespoon olive oil

salt flakes

120 ml extra virgin olive oil

45 ml red wine vinegar

1 garlic clove, finely chopped
  or crushed

handful of flat-leaf parsley leaves,
  finely shredded, plus a few
  extra leaves

handful of coriander leaves,
  finely shredded

200 g smoked mozzarella
  or scamorza, broken
  into 1 cm chunks

freshly ground black pepper

I love the sweet taste and elegant look of long capsicums, otherwise known as bullhorn capsicums or peppers. If you can't find them, regular red capsicums would also be delicious here. You should be able to find good-quality smoked mozzarella in most specialist delis or cheese shops. Otherwise, use buffalo mozzarella, which is superior to mozzarella made from cow's milk, and to my mind is well worth the extra pennies.

This is fantastic served simply with rocket, but would also work well piled onto thick slices of sourdough bread as a tartine.

Preheat the oven to 250°C.

Place the capsicums in a baking dish or roasting tin, toss with the olive oil and a pinch of salt and roast until blistered and soft, about 15 minutes. Remove the capsicums from the oven and set aside, then reduce the oven temperature to 220°C.

Whisk together the extra virgin olive oil, vinegar, garlic and half of each of the parsley and coriander to make a dressing.

When the capsicums are cool enough to handle, cut along the length of each one to open it up, then remove the seeds. Drizzle a tablespoon of the dressing into the cavity of each capsicum, followed by a quarter of the cheese.

Return the capsicums to the oven and roast for 5 minutes or until the cheese has melted and is lightly browned.

Scatter with the remaining parsley and coriander and a little pepper, then finish with a few parsley leaves. Spoon over any extra dressing and pan juices when serving.

SWEETCORN WITH JALAPENO, LIME & PARMESAN

SERVES 6

6 corn cobs, husks removed

40 g (½ cup) finely grated parmesan

large handful of coriander sprigs

JALAPENO & LIME DRESSING

6 coriander roots, cleaned and roughly chopped

pinch of salt flakes

3 spring onions, cut into thin rings

1 jalapeno chilli, cut into thin rings

juice of 1 lime

60 ml (¼ cup) extra virgin olive oil

This easy sweetcorn makes a great lunchtime treat, and is the perfect addition to roast chicken or grilled fish. To keep things even simpler, forgo the dressing and just squeeze some fresh lime juice over the cooked corn, then scatter with chilli salt (see page 228).

If you have the time and inclination, chargrill or barbecue the corn – or roast it in a 250°C oven for 10 minutes – to give it an extra flavour dimension.

To make the dressing, use a pestle and mortar to pound the coriander roots and salt to a paste. Add the spring onion and jalapeno rings and lightly pound, just to combine. Stir in the lime juice and olive oil.

Cook the corn in plenty of boiling salted water for 10–15 minutes until tender, then drain.

Toss the hot corn in the dressing, then sprinkle liberally with parmesan and coriander sprigs.

82

ROMAN BEANS BRAISED IN OLIVE OIL WITH TOMATO & DILL

SERVES 4–6

600 g roman beans

50 ml olive oil

1 leek, white part only,
    cut into fine rings

salt flakes

10 garlic cloves, thinly sliced

100 ml white wine

2 × 400 g cans diced tomatoes

squeeze of lemon juice, if needed

freshly ground white pepper

handful of chopped dill

Any kind of long beans, such as green beans, bobby beans or wax beans can be used for this if roman beans are unavailable. You can of course serve this hot, but I like it best at room temperature with a sprinkling of chilli salt (see page 228); team with some grilled sardines or roast lamb for a real treat.

Top and tail the beans, stringing them down the side in one movement. Cut them in half on the diagonal (cut any extra-long ones into three).

Heat the olive oil in a saucepan over low heat and gently cook the leek until tender for about 2 minutes. Add a pinch of salt and the garlic and cook for another minute. Add the beans and stir to coat with the oil, then add the wine and increase the heat to medium. Simmer until the wine is reduced to a syrupy glaze.

Add the tomatoes to the pan and simmer for 20 minutes until the beans are tender and the sauce is intense and glossy. Adjust the seasoning with salt and pepper, and add a squeeze of lemon juice if more acidity is needed.

Fold in the chopped dill and serve.

ROAST PUMPKIN, PERSIAN FETA & CHILLI OIL TARTINE

SERVES 4

½ jap pumpkin (about 1.5 kg)

canola oil spray

salt flakes

4 red onions

3 teaspoons ground cumin

freshly ground black pepper

1 preserved lemon quarter, rind only, diced

2 tablespoons extra virgin olive oil, plus extra for brushing

4 thick slices sourdough bread

120 g Persian feta

large handful of pea tendrils or snowpea shoots and chilli oil (see page 226), to serve

There are dark mutterings in the lunchtime queue at Kitchen by Mike on the days we don't offer this simple open sandwich. The sweet pumpkin is a great foil for the salty feta cheese. If you can't find Persian feta, you can use any feta, or try smoked mozzarella for a change.

Preheat the oven to 220°C.

Cut the pumpkin into wedges, leaving the skin on and seeds in. Place pumpkin, skin side down, on a baking tray, spray with canola oil to coat evenly and sprinkle with salt.

Peel the onions and cut into quarters without cutting all the way through, to keep the layers of the onion together while they cook. Place on another baking tray, sprinkle with the cumin and season with salt and pepper. Drizzle with the olive oil and gently toss to coat the onion.

Roast the onion and pumpkin for 30–45 minutes or until both are very tender – the onion should be lightly caramelised and the tips of the pumpkin wedges should be slightly burnt. Remove from the oven and scatter the onion with the preserved lemon rind.

Brush the bread with olive oil and toast on the barbecue or under the grill. Scoop the pumpkin flesh from the skin and squash onto the toast. Scatter the onion on top, crumble over the cheese and top with some pea tendrils. Drizzle with a little chilli oil, then season with salt and pepper and serve.

FIGS, PROSCIUTTO, YOUNG PECORINO & HONEY ON TOAST

SERVES 4

4 thick slices sourdough bread

olive oil, for brushing

180 g prosciutto, finely sliced

1½ tablespoons extra virgin
   olive oil

1 tablespoon honey

40 g wild rocket

6 figs, cut into sixths

salt flakes and freshly ground
   black pepper

180 g young pecorino

handful of basil leaves

This is just delicious when the figs are on song. When I choose figs at the market, I always look for a small amount of syrup oozing from the core on their undersides – this is a good indication that they will be really ripe and juicy. Young pecorino has a similar texture to firm mozzarella and packs a lovely salty flavour to balance the sweetness of the figs and honey; aged pecorino, however, is more like parmesan, making it a little dry for this. A better alternative would be a semi-firm cheese, such as gruyere, comte or tomme, but if using one of these, season the tartine with some extra salt flakes to balance the sweetness.

Brush the bread with olive oil and toast on the barbecue or under the grill. Place a ruffled slice of prosciutto on each piece.

Whisk together the extra virgin olive oil and honey to make a dressing. Place the rocket and figs in a bowl, season with salt and pepper and pour over half of the dressing. Toss well and pile on top of the prosciutto.

Shave or thinly slice the pecorino and arrange on top, then scatter with basil leaves. Drizzle over a little more dressing and season with salt and pepper.

PISSALADIERE

SERVES 4—6

3 red capsicums (peppers)

50 g anchovy fillets, cut into
    thin strips

50 g olives, ideally taggiasche,
    stones removed

ONION CONFIT WITH CAPERS & THYME

2 tablespoons salted baby capers

60 ml (¼ cup) olive oil

50 g anchovy fillets, chopped

handful of thyme leaves

1 kg brown onions, finely sliced

pinch of salt flakes

SHORTCRUST PASTRY

200 g plain flour, sifted

125 g chilled salted butter,
    diced

Pissaladiere is truly one of my favourite things. I use a shortcrust pastry known as 'pate brisee', as I adore its crumbly texture (if you make a double batch, you can freeze half and have the makings of your next pissaladiere or pie crust ready to go), but many people use a brioche or pizza dough. Either way, the sweet stewed onions and salty anchovies are a match made in heaven. Do make the effort to remove the olive stones so you won't have to stop and start mid-mouthful or risk dental damage! This is the pizza of southern France, so a glass of pale, dry rose is a must here.

For the onion confit, soak the capers in warm water for 20 minutes, then drain and pat dry. Heat the olive oil in a heavy-based saucepan over low heat and add the capers, anchovies and thyme. Sweat slowly for 2 minutes until the anchovies have melted. Add the onion and a pinch of salt, then cook slowly until the onion is translucent and all the excess liquid has evaporated – this will take at least 1 hour.

While the onion is cooking, make the pastry. Rub the butter into the flour with your fingertips or pulse in a food processor until the mixture resembles fine breadcrumbs. Gradually add just enough cold water (about 2 tablespoons) to form a dough. Wrap the pastry in cling film and rest in the fridge for 30 minutes.

Preheat the oven to 180°C and line a large baking tray with baking paper.

Place the capsicums in a small baking dish or roasting tin and roast for 20 minutes or until blistered and soft to touch. Place in a clean plastic bag to sweat as they cool.

Place the pastry between two sheets of baking paper and roll out a 2 mm thick sheet of pastry to fit your baking tray. Remove the top layer of paper and prick the pastry all over with a fork. Transfer the pastry to the prepared baking tray and bake for 15 minutes until golden and crisp. Keep an eye on the pastry as it cooks – if it starts to rise, open the oven door, gently push the pastry down and reduce the oven temperature to 170°C for the remainder of the cooking time. Remove and set aside to firm slightly.

When the roasted capsicums are cool enough to handle, remove the skin and seeds, then cut into 5 mm strips.

Spread the pastry with the onion confit. Arrange alternate lines of anchovy and capsicum strips on top to make a lattice pattern, then place an olive in the centre of each diamond. Return to the oven for 5 minutes, just to bring all of the flavours together.

Serve the pissaladiere at room temperature, cutting it carefully with a chef's knife and using a sawing action as the pastry will be very crumbly.

BLUE MACKEREL TAGINE WITH COUSCOUS

SERVES 4

2 tablespoons olive oil

4 carrots, diced

2 onions, diced

5 garlic cloves, thinly sliced

about 200 g (⅔ cup) chermoula
 (see page 232)

1 tablespoon honey

200 g cherry tomatoes

2 litres fish stock (see page 242)
 or water

salt flakes and lemon juice,
 to taste

8 blue mackerel fillets, pin-boned

1 preserved lemon quarter,
 rind only, finely chopped

40 g snowpeas (mangetout),
 topped and tailed

½ bunch coriander, leaves picked
 and stalks very finely sliced

harissa (see page 233), to serve

COUSCOUS

300 ml stock or water

150 g instant couscous

30 ml olive oil

Leatherjacket or whiting make good substitutes if blue mackerel is unavailable. Once you've made the chermoula, this recipe couldn't be more straightforward – and the rest of the chermoula is great to have on hand. Covered with a film of oil in a sterilised jar, it will keep for up to 3 months in the fridge, and can be used for marinating chicken or fish before cooking or served as a dip with crudites.

Heat the olive oil in a tagine or heavy-based saucepan over low–medium heat and fry the carrot, onion and garlic until tender. Add half of the chermoula and cook until aromatic, then stir in the honey to caramelise. Add the tomatoes and stock or water and bring to the boil, then turn the heat down to a slow simmer and cook for 1 hour. Check the seasoning and balance with salt and lemon juice.

Meanwhile, preheat the oven to 220°C. Lay each fish fillet flesh side up on your benchtop and use your fingers to check all the bones are gone. Arrange some chopped preserved lemon rind and sliced coriander stalk down the middle of each fish fillet, then roll up (like a roll-mop herring) and secure with a toothpick. Smear the fish with the remaining chermoula, then place in a large roasting tin or baking dish and bake until half-cooked, about 5 minutes. Pour the tagine over the fish, add the snowpeas and bake for another 5 minutes or until the fish is cooked.

To prepare the couscous, bring the stock or water to the boil in a saucepan with a tight-fitting lid. Rub the couscous thoroughly with the olive oil until well coated. Add the couscous to the pan and stir once, then immediately cover with the lid and remove from the heat. Leave covered for 5 minutes, then fork through the grains to separate them and make the couscous fluffy.

Scatter the tagine with coriander leaves, then serve in bowls with couscous and harissa.

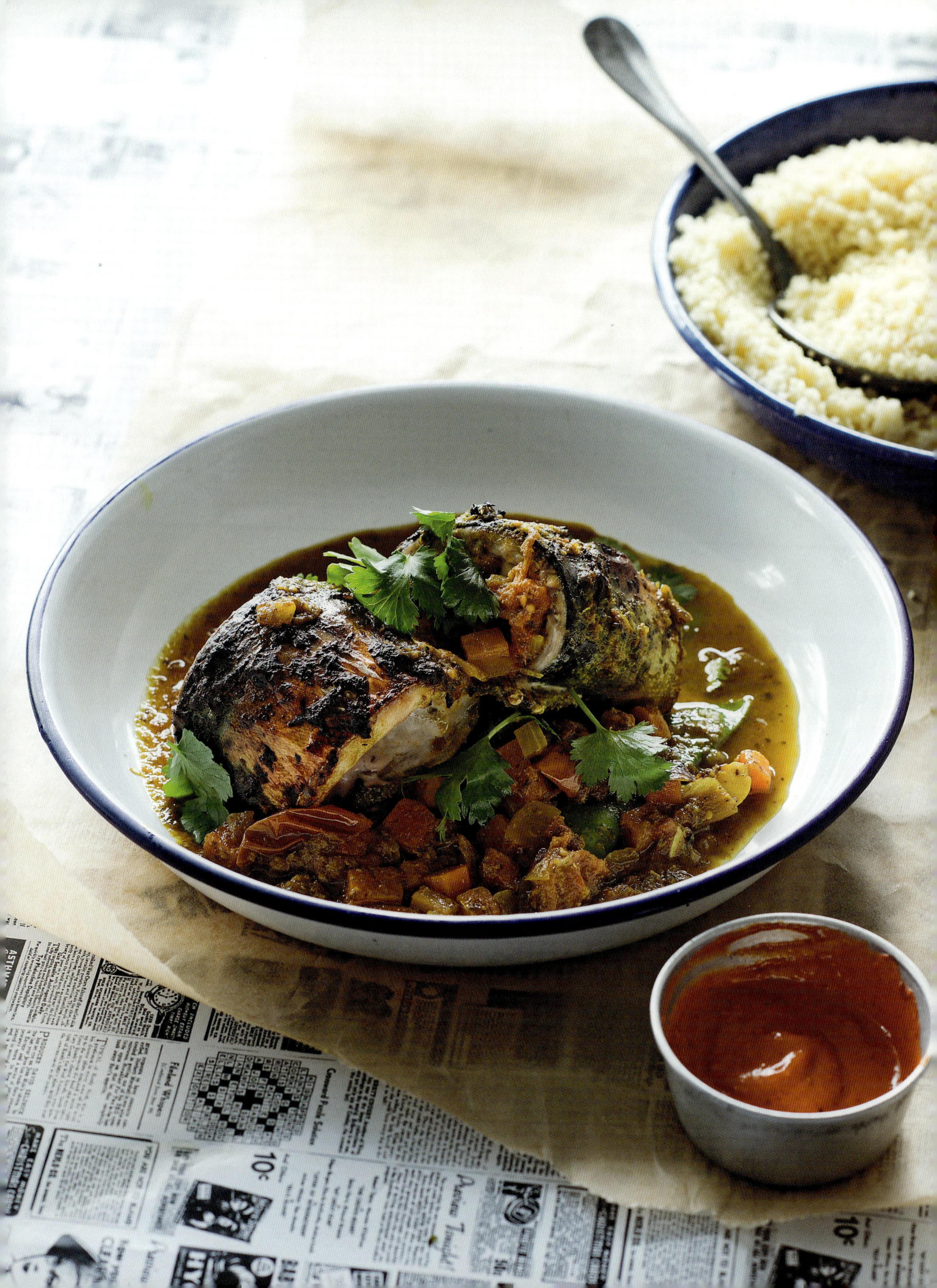
10¢
10¢

KOULIBIAC

SERVES 10

200 g baby spinach leaves

4 tablespoons olive oil

1.2 kg salmon or ocean trout fillet, pin-boned

100 g button mushrooms, finely sliced

handful of flat-leaf parsley leaves, chopped

handful of dill leaves, chopped

freshly ground black pepper

5 hard-boiled eggs, peeled and cut into quarters

500 g puff pastry

2 egg yolks

4 tablespoons cream

100 ml warm clarified or melted butter

RICE PILAF

1 tablespoon butter

3 red shallots, finely chopped

5 garlic cloves, finely chopped

salt flakes

100 g basmati rice

½ teaspoon sweet paprika

300 ml stock or water

Sometimes spelt coulibiac, this is a Russian version of fish pie containing salmon or ocean trout, rice pilaf, mushrooms, spinach, hard-boiled egg and herbs such as dill and parsley, all wrapped in puff pastry and baked. Serve with a large green salad and some boiled potatoes.

For the rice pilaf, choose a 1-litre saucepan with a tight-fitting lid. Melt the butter in the pan over low heat and gently sweat the shallot and garlic with a pinch of salt until soft and translucent. Add the rice and paprika and stir for 30 seconds to coat the rice.

Pour in the stock and bring to the boil. Stir once to make sure the rice isn't catching on the bottom of the pan, then cover the pan with the lid. Turn the heat down to the lowest setting and simmer very slowly for 15 minutes, then remove from the heat. Leave the pilaf to sit for 10 minutes without lifting the lid – don't be tempted to take a peek, or steam will escape and this will affect the cooking of the top layer of rice. After the time is up, remove the lid and fork through the rice to fluff up the grains. Transfer to a large bowl and leave to cool slightly.

While the rice is cooking, blanch the spinach leaves in boiling water for 5 seconds just to wilt, then drain, squeezing out as much water as possible. Spread out the leaves in a single layer on a large sheet of cling film.

Heat 1 tablespoon of the olive oil in a non-stick frying pan and pan-fry the salmon or trout so it is golden on the outside but still rare in the centre. Remove from the pan and allow to cool, then remove the skin and flake the flesh into large chunks, discarding any stray bones.

Add the remaining 3 tablespoons of olive oil to the frying pan and saute the mushrooms until tender.

Tip the mushrooms into the rice pilaf, stir in the parsley and dill, and adjust the seasoning with salt and pepper. Gently fold in the flaked fish and hard-boiled egg quarters.

Carefully spoon the rice mixture down the centre of the spinach leaves, then use the cling film to ease the spinach leaves around the filling, rolling so that the filling is entirely enclosed in a layer of spinach and is shaped like a large sausage. Place in the fridge to chill while you roll out the pastry.

Line a large baking tray with baking paper. Place the pastry on a lightly floured benchtop and roll out three-quarters of it to make a sheet about 45 cm × 35 cm. (Keep the rest of the pastry for the lattice decoration later.)

In a small bowl, lightly beat the egg yolks with the cream to make an eggwash.

V

Remove the rice 'sausage' from the fridge and carefully remove the cling film, then place on one of the long edges of the pastry sheet. Gently roll the pastry around the filling, enclosing it completely. Seal the join with eggwash and place on the prepared baking tray, seam-side down.

Roll out the remaining quarter of the pastry to a 5 mm thickness, then cut into strips about 1 cm wide. Brush the top of the koulibiac with eggwash and lay the strips of pastry on top in a diamond lattice pattern. Brush again with eggwash and chill in the fridge for 30 minutes.

Preheat the oven to 250°C. Brush the koulibiac with eggwash one more time and use a fork to prick the pastry in three places to allow the steam to escape during baking. Transfer to the oven and bake for 10 minutes, then reduce the oven temperature to 200°C and bake until the pastry is golden and the filling is hot, about another 10 minutes. Remember that the filling is already cooked – the idea is to cook the pastry quickly so it forms a golden crust and doesn't go soggy from the steam of the filling.

Remove the koulibiac from the oven and carefully slide onto a platter or chopping board. Use the tip of a funnel to poke 3 holes along the length of the koulibiac, then pour in the warm clarified or melted butter through the funnel, distributing it evenly between the holes. Let the koulibiac sit for 5 minutes before slicing and serving.

96

ROAST CHICKEN VINAIGRETTE

SERVES 4

1 garlic bulb, cut in half

1 × 1.8 kg free-range chicken

2 tablespoons extra virgin olive oil

salt flakes

6 baby 'pencil' leeks or 1–2 regular leeks, white parts only, well washed

125 ml (½ cup) white wine

200 g green beans, tailed

80 g hazelnuts

WINE & HERB VINAIGRETTE

4 golden shallots, finely diced

2 tablespoons white wine

2 tablespoons red wine vinegar

125 ml (½ cup) extra virgin olive oil

handful of finely chopped flat-leaf parsley

handful of finely chopped tarragon

handful of finely chopped chives

handful of finely chopped chervil

freshly ground white pepper, to taste

This French bistro classic is now my go-to roast chicken recipe. I like to truss the chicken so it cooks more evenly, but this is not essential. The dressing is a play on the mignonette sauce that traditionally accompanies oysters, but with the addition of fresh soft herbs and olive oil, it becomes a delicious vinaigrette. You can use any combination of seasonal vegetables in place of the green beans and leeks – the important thing is to aim for something light and textural that will complement this warm salad, rather than overwhelm it. If you have a nut allergy, croutons make a good substitute for the crunch of the hazelnuts, and they'll also soak up some of the tasty juices. For a more substantial meal, add some roast potatoes or boiled new potatoes.

Preheat the oven to 220°C.

Place the garlic in the cavity of the chicken and rub the chicken all over with olive oil and salt.

Cut the baby leeks in half crossways to give 12 nice lengths. If using regular leeks, cut them into 8 cm lengths. Place the leeks in the base of a roasting tin to act as a trivet for the chicken. Sit the chicken on top of the leeks and drizzle over the wine.

Roast the chicken in the oven, with its legs towards the back, for 25 minutes, then reduce the temperature to 180°C and roast for another 20 minutes. To check if the chicken is done, grab a drumstick and twist gently – it should easily slip out of the joint and come away from the thigh.

Remove the tin from the oven, scatter the beans around the chook and spoon over some of the pan juices.

Return the tin to the oven, then turn the oven off and leave the door ajar. Let the chicken rest in the cooling oven for 15 minutes (the residual heat will be just enough to lightly cook the beans).

Meanwhile, to make the vinaigrette, combine all the ingredients in a bowl.

Transfer the chicken to a board. Give the roasting tin a gentle shake to coat the soft leeks and al dente beans with the juices, then tilt the tin and carefully tip away the chicken fat, leaving the vegetables and juices in the tin. (If using regular leeks, cut them in half lengthways.)

Cut the chicken into pieces and place on top of the vegetables in the roasting tin, then spoon over the vinaigrette and scatter with the hazelnuts. Leave to sit while you gather everyone around the table, to allow the vinaigrette to mingle with the pan juices. Serve warm.

CHICKEN, AVOCADO & CUCUMBER WRAP

SERVES 4

juice and finely grated zest
of ½ lemon

30 ml extra virgin olive oil

pinch of caster sugar

salt flakes and freshly ground
black pepper

80 g wild rocket

4 flatbread wraps

aioli (see page 230), for spreading

400 g roast chicken meat

2 avocados

CUCUMBER PICKLE

1 small cucumber, thinly sliced

1 teaspoon salt flakes

1 teaspoon caster sugar

125 ml (½ cup) Japanese
rice vinegar

This recipe is perfect for using up leftover roast chicken (see opposite). Any excess cucumber pickle can be kept for a month in a jar in the fridge, and is great with cold meats.

For the cucumber pickle, toss the cucumber with the salt and sugar in a sieve set over a bowl and leave to sit for 30 minutes.

In a bowl, whisk the lemon juice and zest with the olive oil and a pinch each of caster sugar and salt flakes. Add the rocket and toss gently.

Pat the cucumber dry, then tip into a non-reactive bowl and stir in the vinegar.

Lay the flatbread on the bench and spread with aioli. Tear the roast chicken into strips and season well with salt and pepper. Place a row of chicken strips along the centre of the wrap, then top with some rocket and chunks of avocado.

Scatter with cucumber pickle, then roll tightly, folding in the ends as you go, and secure with a strip of greaseproof paper.

Cut in half and eat!

SPIT-ROAST LAMB WITH ROAST PLUMS

SERVES 24

1 × 18 kg whole lamb on a spit (ask your butcher to prepare this for you)

3 bunches thyme

1 bunch rosemary

12 garlic cloves, unpeeled

rosemary tapenade (see page 240), to serve

PROVENCAL BASTING MIXTURE

1.5 litres olive oil

20 garlic cloves, peeled

1 tablespoon cayenne pepper

2 bunches thyme, leaves picked

2 bunches rosemary, leaves picked

500 ml (2 cups) red wine vinegar

2 tablespoons fine salt

ROAST PLUMS

12 blood plums

3 tablespoons olive oil

salt flakes

3 teaspoons vincotto

This is a magnificent way to feed a big gathering, and is perfect for a special occasion. You'll need to order the whole lamb in advance from your butcher, and they can usually help with spit hire as well. An average lamb will yield about a third of its weight in meat, and you should allow about 250 g meat per person, so to calculate the size of lamb you need, multiply 750 g by the number of people.

The tart plums and pungent rosemary tapenade cut through rich meats beautifully, so if you're not up for spit-roasting a whole lamb, try them with a slow-roast lamb shoulder. The roast plums are also lovely with some rocket and crumbled goat's cheese and walnuts as a light salad or served alongside roast duck or goose.

For the provencal basting mixture, blend all the ingredients in an upright blender until smooth.

Make a fire of hardwood logs or charcoal and allow to burn for 2 hours or until there are no more flames and glowing embers have formed. Use a shovel to arrange the embers so that there is more at both ends of the spit (to cook the shoulder and rumps) and less in the centre (to protect the loin, which needs less cooking). Place the coals in rows to one or both sides so there is none directly under the lamb, which could cause a flare up.

Ask your butcher to set the lamb on the spit so the front legs are forward and the hind legs are back. Place the herbs and garlic in the belly cavity and sew up. Place over the coals, start the spit rotating and baste the lamb. Cook slowly, basting regularly, for 4–6 hours or until a probe thermometer inserted near the bone registers 55–60°C.

When the lamb is ready, remove it from the heat and allow to rest for 30 minutes before taking out the spit and supports.

Meanwhile, place the plums in a baking dish or roasting tin, then drizzle with olive oil and season with salt. Roast over the coals for about 15 minutes or until the plums feel soft and their skins start to split. Remove from the coals and allow to rest for 5 minutes, then drizzle with the vincotto.

When you're ready to serve, carve the lamb and arrange on a large platter. Place in the centre of the table, along with the roast plums and the rosemary tapenade, and let people help themselves.

APRICOT TART

SERVES 8

375 g puff pastry

1 egg, beaten

500 g apricots, cut in half
(or quarters, if large) and
stones removed

1 tablespoon caster sugar

1 tablespoon pure icing sugar

50 g apricot jam

thick cream or creme fraiche,
to serve

CREME PATISSIERE

125 ml (½ cup) milk

½ teaspoon vanilla paste

1 egg yolk

1 tablespoon caster sugar

1 tablespoon cornflour

FRANGIPANE

100 g caster sugar

100 g almonds, skin on

100 g chilled unsalted butter,
diced

pinch of fine salt

2 teaspoons brandy

1 egg, lightly beaten

3 teaspoons milk

Like all stonefruit, apricots are at their peak in the hotter months, and
they really shine in this tart. Feel free to use shop-bought puff pastry
here, preferably the sort that comes in a block rather than ready-rolled.
Frangipane and creme patissiere both keep well in the fridge and so can
be made a few days in advance; use the leftover frangipane for the apple
tarte fine on page 190.

Grease a 25 cm tart tin with a removable base. On a lightly floured benchtop,
roll out the pastry to a 3 mm thick circle large enough to fit the tin with a
slight overhang all round. Roll the pastry around the rolling pin and carefully
ease into the prepared tin, using a pastry brush to gently press the pastry
into the corners – do not trim the excess pastry yet. Place the tart shell in
the fridge to rest for 30 minutes.

To make the creme patissiere, bring the milk slowly to the boil with the
vanilla, then remove from the heat. In a small bowl, whisk together the egg
yolk and sugar until the sugar has dissolved and the mixture is pale. Add the
cornflour and whisk until there are no lumps. Pour a spoonful of the vanilla-
infused warm milk into the egg-yolk mixture and whisk until smooth, then
pour back into the saucepan. Place the pan over low heat and simmer for
2 minutes, whisking constantly until the mixture thickens and the cornflour
is cooked and no longer grainy. Remove from the heat and cover with cling
film, pressing it onto the surface to prevent a skin forming, then allow to cool.

Meanwhile, make the frangipane. Blitz 25 g of the sugar with the almonds
in a blender or small food processor until finely ground. Add the butter and
the remaining 75 g of sugar, and process until pale and fluffy. Slowly add
the brandy, followed by the egg and the milk, blending until smooth and well
combined. Whisk half of the frangipane into the cooled creme patissiere.

Preheat the oven to 190°C.

Remove the tart shell from the fridge and trim the overhanging edges of the
pastry, then prick the base all over with a fork. Line with a sheet of baking
paper, then fill with rice, dried beans or pastry weights. Bake the tart shell for
15 minutes until the pastry has set and is starting to colour, then remove the
weights and baking paper and return to the oven for 5 minutes. Brush the tart
shell with the beaten egg and bake for another 5 minutes to seal the pastry.
Remove the tart shell from the oven and reduce the temperature to 170°C.

Toss the apricots with the caster sugar to release their natural juices. Spread
the tart base with a 1 cm layer of the creme patissiere mixture, then arrange
the apricot halves on top, cut side up. Dust with the icing sugar and bake for
45–60 minutes, until the apricots are cooked and slightly burnt around the
edges. Remove the tart from the oven and leave to cool on a wire rack.

When the tart is cool, warm the apricot jam and brush over the top to glaze.
Serve with cream or creme fraiche to balance the sweetness.

CHERRIES WITH KIRSCH GRANITA & WHITE CHOCOLATE SABAYON

SERVES 4

100 g caster sugar
360 g cherries, chilled

KIRSCH GRANITA
180 g cherries
80 ml (⅓ cup) kirsch

WHITE CHOCOLATE SABAYON
3 egg yolks
20 g white chocolate, broken
   into small pieces
40 g creme fraiche

Here is my take on the classic flavours of a Black Forest cake, reimagined for an Australian summer. This is a celebration of the amazing cherries grown around Young in New South Wales, which reach their peak during December. When they are perfect, I love serving them on ice – and that's where the granita comes in, making a tongue-tingling contrast with the warm sabayon. Kirsch, a clear cherry brandy, is available from most bottle shops. Not only is it the perfect foil for the cherries, but the alcohol content will help keep your granita from setting rock-solid.

Place the sugar in a small saucepan with 100 ml of water. Place over medium heat, stirring to dissolve the sugar. Bring the syrup to the boil, then remove from the heat and leave to cool.

For the granita, pit the cherries and remove their stalks, then blend to a puree in a blender or small food processor and pass through a fine-meshed sieve. Measure 80 ml (⅓ cup) of the cherry puree into a bowl and add 80 ml (⅓ cup) of the sugar syrup. Stir in the kirsch, then transfer to a shallow container and freeze for at least 3 hours, scraping the ice crystals with a fork every 30 minutes, until you have a flaky granita.

For the sabayon, place the egg yolks in a heatproof bowl with the remaining 20 ml of syrup. Set over a pan of simmering water and whisk until the mixture is light and airy – when you lift up the whisk, it should leave a ribbon-like trace. Remove from the heat, then fold in the chocolate off the heat, stirring gently until dissolved. Leave to cool, then fold in the creme fraiche just before serving.

To serve, scoop the granita into bowls, top with the chilled cherries and pour over the sabayon.

CREAMY RICE PUDDING WITH POACHED PLUMS

SERVES 4

60 g short-grain rice

160 g caster sugar

1 vanilla bean, split and
   seeds scraped

1 cinnamon quill

½ teaspoon freshly grated nutmeg

360 ml milk

90 ml evaporated milk

90 ml double cream or
   creme fraiche

8 plums

juice of 1 lemon

Yummy and simple, rice pudding works best with short-grain pudding rice. If you can't find it, try using arborio or sushi rice. After the plums have been cooked, any leftover poaching syrup can be mixed with an equal quantity of red wine to make a granita: simply freeze in a shallow container for at least 3 hours, scraping the ice crystals with a fork every 30 minutes, until you have a flaky granita.

This creamy rice pudding is delicious served with a dollop of good jam or some baked rhubarb (see page 51) instead of the poached plums.

Place the rice, 60 g of the sugar, the vanilla seeds and pod, cinnamon quill, nutmeg and milk in a heavy-based saucepan over low heat and simmer slowly for about an hour or until the rice is tender, stirring regularly so the rice doesn't stick.

Add the evaporated milk and simmer for another 10 minutes, then transfer to a bowl and leave to cool. When the rice pudding is cold, remove the vanilla pod, fold through the cream or creme fraiche and leave to set in the fridge for a couple of hours – or overnight, if you have time.

Meanwhile, cut four of the plums in half and remove the stones, then roughly chop the flesh. Place in a blender or small food processor with the lemon juice and 400 ml of water and puree until very smooth. Add the remaining 100 g sugar and whiz briefly to combine, then pour into a small heavy-based saucepan that will snugly hold the four whole plums.

Remove the stems from the whole plums and trim their bases so they will sit flat. Place in the pan with the plum puree and top up with water to cover, if necessary. Bring to a simmer and cook for 15 minutes or until the plums are fork-tender. Remove from the heat and leave the plums to cool to room temperature in their syrup.

Take the plums out of the syrup, then place the pan of syrup over medium heat and simmer until reduced by half. Slip the skins off the plums and return them to the reduced syrup, then chill in the fridge until needed.

Serve the rice pudding in bowls or glasses with a whole plum and a little of the plum syrup spooned over.

SPICY PUMPKIN TEA CAKE

MAKES 1 LOAF

¼ jap pumpkin (about 750 g)
canola oil spray
250 g (1⅔ cups) plain flour
1½ teaspoons baking powder
½ teaspoon bicarbonate of soda
1½ tablespoons ground cinnamon
½ teaspoon ground cardamom
½ teaspoon ground ginger
2 teaspoons freshly grated nutmeg
¼ teaspoon ground cloves
250 ml (1 cup) vegetable oil
2 tablespoons chopped glace
    ginger in syrup
275 g (1¼ cups) caster sugar
¾ teaspoon salt flakes
3 eggs
pure icing sugar, for dusting

You'll need to prepare the pumpkin for this cake the day before, so the cooked pumpkin has time to hang and drain overnight before being pureed. This will give you an intense-flavoured puree that will make all the difference (and any leftover pumpkin puree makes a delicious side dish with roast chicken or pork). This tea cake is delicious by itself – or dress it up a bit with some creme fraiche and summer berries, and perhaps some pecans for crunch.

The day before you want to bake the cake, preheat the oven to 220°C.

Cut the pumpkin into wedges, leaving the skin on and seeds in. Place the pumpkin, skin side down, on a baking tray and coat evenly with canola spray. Roast the pumpkin for 30–45 minutes or until very soft. When it is cool enough to handle, scrape the flesh from the skin and remove all the seeds. Place the pumpkin in a fine-meshed sieve – without pressing down on it – and suspend over a bowl, then leave in the fridge overnight.

In the morning, you will find a pool of orange liquid in the bowl under the sieve. Discard the liquid and mash the dry pumpkin flesh to a smooth puree.

Preheat the oven to 175°C. Spray a loaf tin with canola oil and line the base with baking paper.

Sift the flour, baking powder, bicarbonate of soda and spices into a bowl and set aside.

Place 275 g of the pumpkin puree, together with the vegetable oil, glace ginger, caster sugar and salt, in the bowl of an electric mixer fitted with the paddle attachment. Mix until smooth, then add the eggs one at a time, beating well between each addition. Add the flour mixture and mix on low speed to combine, then increase the speed and beat until smooth.

Pour the batter into the prepared loaf tin and smooth the surface. Bake for 45–60 minutes or until a skewer inserted in the centre comes out clean.

Leave the loaf to cool in the tin for 20 minutes, then transfer to a wire rack to cool completely. Dust with icing sugar before serving.

CHAPTER

3

AUT

TOASTED MUESLI

MAKES ABOUT 1 KG

100 g honey, warmed
   to make it runny
100 ml extra virgin olive oil
3 teaspoons ground cinnamon
250 g rolled oats (not instant)
160 g raisins
100 g almonds, skin on,
   roughly chopped
100 g unsalted pistachios,
   roughly chopped
100 g dried apricots,
   roughly chopped
100 g linseeds
100 g pumpkin seeds
30 g sesame seeds
1 tablespoon chia seeds

This is a basic recipe that is very easy to customise to your liking. For example, replace some of the nuts with pecans, or use maple syrup instead of honey. You can serve it with milk or yoghurt, or even as a topping over stewed fruit.

Preheat the oven to 130°C. Line a baking tray with baking paper.

Mix together the honey, oil and cinnamon in a bowl, add the oats and toss to coat. Scatter the oats over the prepared tray and bake for 30–45 minutes or until golden. Remove from the oven and leave to cool completely.

Combine the cooled oats with the remaining ingredients, then store in an airtight container for up to 1 month.

SOURDOUGH PANCAKES WITH LEMON CURD

SERVES 4

280 g plain flour

3 teaspoons baking powder

60 g caster sugar

10 eggs, separated

240 g sourdough starter
(see page 202)

400 ml milk

140 g butter, melted, plus extra
for brushing

vegetable oil, melted butter or
canola oil spray, for frying

lemon curd (see page 219),
to serve

pure icing sugar, for dusting

This is the big daddy of pancake recipes. The sourdough contributes a lovely acidity reminiscent of real buttermilk, and the slow fermentation (ideally overnight) gives the pancakes a full flavour and a firm but fluffy texture. Make sure you don't over-whip your egg whites – if they are too stiff, it will be impossible to fold them in to make a smooth batter without knocking out all the air. If you want to make these pancakes for breakfast, prepare the batter the night before, then leave it to prove in the fridge overnight.

Combine the flour, baking powder and sugar in a bowl.

In a jug, whisk together the egg yolks, sourdough starter and milk. Add the tepid melted butter and whisk to combine, then add to the dry ingredients and beat to a soft, thick batter. Cover and leave to rest in the fridge for at least an hour, or overnight. Keep the egg whites refrigerated too.

Shortly before you're ready to eat, whisk the egg whites until soft peaks form, then gently fold through the batter.

Brush a large non-stick frying pan with a thin film of oil or melted butter (or spray with canola oil) and heat over medium heat. When the pan is hot, pour ladlefuls of batter into the pan and cook for 1–1½ minutes. Flip the pancakes over and cook for 1 minute more until the underside is firm and sealed. Transfer to a warm plate and brush with a little extra melted butter, then cover to keep warm while you cook the rest of the pancakes, brushing each one with butter to keep it moist and placing them on top of each other to make a stack. This amount of batter should give you about 12–16 fat, fluffy pancakes.

Stack the pancakes on four plates. Serve warm with a dollop of lemon curd and a dusting of icing sugar.

118

BAKED BEANS WITH BACON & A POACHED EGG

SERVES 4

250 g dried cannellini beans
1 teaspoon bicarbonate of soda
1 small carrot, diced
3 garlic cloves, minced
1 bay leaf
small handful of parsley stalks
salt flakes
8 slices bacon
1 tablespoon fresh breadcrumbs
1–2 teaspoons white wine vinegar
4 eggs
4 thick slices sourdough bread
butter, for spreading
chilli oil (see page 226), to serve

TOMATO SAUCE

60 ml (¼ cup) extra virgin olive oil
1 small onion, finely chopped
3 garlic cloves, thinly sliced
1 small carrot, cut into 1 cm dice
1 small celery stick, diced
2 teaspoons smoked sweet
   Spanish paprika
2 teaspoons sweet Hungarian
   paprika
1 chipotle chilli, soaked, seeded
   and chopped
100 ml white wine
2 tablespoons black treacle
1 kg canned tomatoes
¼ bunch thyme, leaves picked
4 sprigs rosemary, leaves picked
   and chopped
salt flakes and freshly ground
   black pepper
½ bunch dill, leaves picked and
   chopped

Dried cannellini beans need to be soaked overnight – and baked beans are always better the next day, so plan ahead. The chipotle chilli gives the sauce a wonderful smokiness, but you could just spike the sauce with a little more smoked paprika instead: it comes in sweet, mild and hot varieties, so choose wisely, depending on your heat threshold!

Soak the beans overnight in 1 litre (4 cups) of water with the bicarbonate of soda. The next day, drain the beans and rinse well, then place in a saucepan, cover with fresh water and bring to the boil. Reduce the heat and simmer for 10 minutes, then drain and rinse again. Return the beans to the pan and pour in enough cold water to cover by 5 cm. Bring to a simmer, skimming any froth from the surface, then add the carrot, garlic, bay leaf and parsley stalks. Cover with a circle of baking paper and simmer very slowly for 1½ hours or until tender, skimming occasionally. Remove the pan from the heat and season with salt, then let the beans cool in their cooking liquid (store in the fridge if you want to bake the beans the next day).

Preheat the oven to 140°C. To make the tomato sauce for the beans, heat the oil in a large flameproof casserole with a lid over medium heat. Add the onion, garlic, carrot and celery and cook until softened, then add the paprika and chilli and cook until aromatic. Pour in the wine and simmer until reduced by half. Stir in the treacle, and then the tomatoes, thyme and rosemary, and simmer for 20 minutes or until the liquid has thickened and reduced by half. Add the drained beans to the sauce and simmer for a minute, then cover the casserole with the lid and transfer to the oven. Bake for 1 hour or until the beans are supple and caramelised around the edges. Season to taste with salt and pepper, add the chopped dill and leave to sit for 5–10 minutes.

Meanwhile, fry the bacon to your liking, then drain on paper towel. Reheat the bacon fat in the pan and fry the breadcrumbs until golden.

Bring a deep pan of water to the boil (I find the deeper the pan, the better the poached egg, as the egg grows a tail as it cooks and assumes a lovely, ghost-like form), then add 1 teaspoon of vinegar and 2 teaspoons of salt per litre of water. Crack each egg into a cup. Turn the heat down so the water is just simmering, then stir the water in one direction to form a vortex. Slip the eggs, one at a time, into the vortex and allow to slowly circle down to the bottom of the pan. The eggs will float to the top when they are ready, about 2 minutes. A perfectly poached egg should feel like a balloon – soft but resilient. Remove from the pan and drain on paper towel.

Toast the bread and spread generously with butter. To serve, spoon a pile of beans onto each plate and top with two slices of bacon. Carefully place a poached egg on top, then scatter with the fried breadcrumbs and drizzle with a little chilli oil. Serve with the hot buttered toast.

120

QUINCE & ALMOND MUFFINS

MAKES 6

325 g plain flour

2 teaspoons baking powder

1½ teaspoons bicarbonate of soda

pinch of fine salt

165 g butter, softened

130 ml vegetable oil

300 g caster sugar

4 eggs

150 ml buttermilk

180 g quince jam, preferably homemade (see page 224)

120 g marzipan, grated

30 g slivered almonds, toasted

pure icing sugar, for dusting

Using a combination of butter and oil in the batter helps to keep these muffins moist and soft, and also prolongs their shelf-life – they'll keep for 3 days in an airtight container. Feel free to substitute the quince jam with your favourite jam.

Preheat the oven to 180°C. Line a six-hole muffin tray with paper cases.

Sift the flour, baking powder, bicarbonate of soda and salt into a bowl and set aside.

In an electric mixer fitted with the paddle attachment, mix the butter, oil and sugar until smooth and fluffy and the sugar has dissolved. Add the eggs one at a time, mixing well after each addition. Slowly add the buttermilk, along with ½ cup of the flour mixture and mix until smooth.

Remove the bowl from the mixer and fold in the remaining flour mixture with a spatula, being careful not to over-mix, which will make the muffins tough. Lightly fold three-quarters of the jam and three-quarters of the marzipan into the batter, to create a ripple effect, then spoon evenly into the muffin cases.

Bake for 20 minutes or until a skewer inserted in the centre comes out clean. Cool in the tin for 15 minutes, then transfer the muffins to a wire rack and leave to cool completely.

When the muffins are cool, top each one with a dollop of the remaining jam and a sprinkling of the remaining marzipan. Scatter with the slivered almonds and finish with a dusting of icing sugar.

CEP MUSHROOM & CHESTNUT SOUP WITH GREEN APPLE & CINNAMON

SERVES 4

40 g dried cep mushrooms

80 g butter

1 small leek, white part only, cut into fine rings

1 small onion, roughly chopped

5 garlic cloves, finely chopped

250 g peeled chestnuts

100 ml cream

salt flakes and freshly ground white pepper

1 granny smith apple

½ teaspoon ground cinnamon

juice of ½ lemon

1 tablespoon creme fraiche

Known as ceps in France and porcini in Italy, *Boletus edulis* are highly prized mushrooms. Any of the precious harvest not sold fresh is thinly sliced and dried, and their intense flavour makes them a formidable ally in the kitchen. If you're not up for roasting and peeling your own chestnuts, look for peeled chestnuts – either frozen or in vacuum-sealed packs – at good delis. Granny smith or another sharp-flavoured apple is ideal to help cut through this rich and creamy, belly-warming soup.

Soak the mushrooms in 500 ml (2 cups) of hot water for 30 minutes or until soft. Lift out the mushrooms, then strain the liquid through a muslin-lined sieve to remove any grit, reserving the soaking liquid as well as the mushrooms.

Melt 20 g of the butter in a large heavy-based saucepan over medium heat Add the leek, onion and garlic and cook for 5 minutes or until translucent. Add the mushrooms and chestnuts, along with the reserved mushroom soaking liquid and 500 ml (2 cups) of water. Simmer for 30 minutes or until the chestnuts are soft.

Puree the soup in an upright blender until very smooth and return to the saucepan. Stir in the cream, then gently reheat and season to taste with salt and pepper.

Meanwhile, peel and core the apple and cut into 5 mm dice. Melt the remaining 60 g of butter in a small frying pan over high heat and let it start to foam and go a light brown colour. Add the apple and cinnamon and saute until slightly softened, then squeeze over the lemon juice.

Ladle the soup into warm bowls. Spoon the apple and brown butter over the soup and finish with a swirl of creme fraiche. Serve immediately.

122

HOT-SMOKED OCEAN TROUT WITH BABY BEETS, SORREL & WALNUTS

SERVES 4

200 g baby beetroot

200 g golden beetroot

40 g baby beetroot leaves
or chard leaves

40 g walnuts, toasted then
broken into large pieces

1 punnet baby sorrel, leaves
picked

freshly ground black pepper

fresh horseradish and horseradish
cream (see page 233), to serve

HOT-SMOKED OCEAN TROUT

3 heaped tablespoons jasmine tea

3 heaped tablespoons brown sugar

3 heaped tablespoons jasmine rice

400 g treacle-cured ocean trout
(see page 28)

CIDER VINAIGRETTE

1 tablespoon apple cider vinegar

3 tablespoons grapeseed oil

1 teaspoon honey

1 teaspoon wholegrain mustard

A fillet cut from the centre of the fish is best here, as fillets from nearer the tail end will cook unevenly and too quickly for this recipe. Be sure to open all the windows before you start – and, if you can, temporarily disarm your smoke alarm, to avoid having to reset it or pay the fire department for a call-out!

For the hot-smoked ocean trout, choose a lidded saucepan large enough to hold a small wire cake rack. Shape a sheet of foil into a shallow bowl that will fit inside the saucepan and place in the base of the pan. Mix together the tea, sugar and rice and place in the foil bowl, then sit the cake rack on top. Heat over medium heat until the tea mixture is smoking, then place the fish on the rack, skin-side down. Cover with the lid and smoke for 2 minutes, then remove from the heat and allow the fish to cool for 3 minutes before lifting off the lid. Check the fish – it should still be slightly pink in the middle. Remove from the pan and leave to cool to room temperature.

To make the vinaigrette, whisk together all the ingredients in a small bowl.

Preheat the oven to 180°C.

Wrap the beets in foil and roast for 45 minutes or until tender. When cool enough to handle, peel off the skins and dress the beets with half of the vinaigrette. Gently toss through the beetroot or chard leaves, then arrange the salad on serving plates.

Flake the smoked trout over the salad, then scatter over the walnuts and sorrel. Drizzle over the remaining vinaigrette and season with pepper, then finish with freshly grated horseradish. Serve with horseradish cream on the side.

SPICED CAULIFLOWER & CHICKPEA SALAD WITH LABNEH

SERVES 4

50 g dried chickpeas

pinch of bicarbonate of soda

50 g salt flakes

1 cauliflower, broken into florets

100 ml extra virgin olive oil

2 red onions, sliced

2 tablespoons curry powder

2 teaspoons ground turmeric

2 teaspoons ground coriander

½ teaspoon ground cinnamon

2 tablespoons ground cumin

2 tablespoons fennel seeds

1 teaspoon ground ginger

2 tablespoons brown mustard seeds

1 tablespoon smoked sweet paprika

½ teaspoon ground cloves

1 teaspoon ground cardamom

75 g (½ cup) raisins, soaked in 125 ml (½ cup) hot water

70 g (½ cup) hazelnuts, toasted and cracked

1 bunch coriander, broken into sprigs

1 bunch mint, leaves picked

50 g baby spinach

100 g labneh (see page 212)

15 ml coconut vinegar

Labneh is like a very mild cheese, made simply by draining yoghurt for a time. It can take several days for the labneh to reach the right texture, so start well ahead of time. The day before, you'll also need to soak the chickpeas and brine the cauliflower.

Coconut vinegar is available from Asian food shops, but if you don't want to buy a whole bottle just for this, you could use good-quality rice vinegar or white wine vinegar.

Soak the chickpeas overnight in 1 litre (4 cups) of water with the bicarbonate of soda.

In a non-reactive bowl, dissolve the salt in 1 litre of water to make a brine. Add the cauliflower and weight it down with a plate to keep it submerged in the brine, then leave overnight in the fridge.

The next day, drain the chickpeas and rinse well, then place in a saucepan, cover with fresh water and bring to the boil. Reduce the heat and simmer for 10 minutes, then drain and rinse again. Return the chickpeas to the saucepan and pour in enough cold water to cover by 5 cm, then simmer for 1½ hours or until tender, skimming any froth from the surface. Remove the pan from the heat and season with salt, then let the chickpeas cool in their cooking liquid.

Preheat the oven to 250°C.

Drain the cauliflower and pat dry, then toss with half of the olive oil, onion and all the spices. Place in a roasting tin and roast for 15 minutes or until caramelised. Remove from the oven and set aside to cool.

Remove the cauliflower and onion from the roasting tin and pour the cooking juices into a small bowl. Add the remaining olive oil and the coconut vinegar and whisk together.

Return the cauliflower and onion to the tin. Add the raisins, hazelnuts, coriander, mint and spinach, then toss gently with the dressing. Transfer to a bowl, scatter with blobs of labneh and serve.

ORIENTAL MUSHROOM SALAD WITH RADISH & CRESS

SERVES 4

1 punnet daikon cress, picked

1 tablespoon white truffle oil

1 bunch radishes, ideally French breakfast variety, cut into quarters

1 punnet purple shiso cress, picked

small handful of coriander leaves

¼ teaspoon black sesame seeds

MARINATED MUSHROOMS & CUCUMBER

60 ml (¼ cup) peanut or grapeseed oil

60 g ginger, cut into fine julienne strips

5 garlic cloves, finely chopped

1 long cucumber, peeled, seeds removed and cut into batons

80 g shiitake mushrooms, stalks removed, caps sliced

80 g oyster mushrooms, trimmed and sliced

80 g shimeji mushrooms, stalks trimmed

250 ml (1 cup) mirin

160 ml (⅔ cup) light soy sauce

80 ml (⅓ cup) Japanese rice vinegar

80 g enoki mushrooms, stalks trimmed

This is a great salad to celebrate mushrooms in autumn, and is equally delicious served warm with some steamed sushi rice. The mushrooms and cucumber are best left to marinate overnight.

Truffle oil is available from specialist food shops – just remember it has an intense flavour, so add a little at a time and taste as you go. If you can't find both kinds of cress, feel free to use more of what you can get, or even some small leaves of coriander or mint.

To make the marinated mushrooms and cucumber, heat the oil in a frying pan over medium heat, then add the ginger and garlic and cook until softened. Add the cucumber and toss for 30 seconds. Add the shiitake, oyster and shimeji mushrooms and lightly saute for 2 minutes. Add the mirin, soy sauce and vinegar and simmer until reduced by half, then remove the pan from the heat and stir in the enoki mushrooms. Transfer to a non-reactive container, cover and leave to marinate in the fridge overnight.

Place the daikon cress in a pile on four plates. Stir the truffle oil through the marinated mushrooms and cucumber, then mix with the radishes, shiso cress and coriander. Arrange on top of the daikon cress, drizzling over some of the juices. Sprinkle with the sesame seeds and serve immediately.

ANCHOVY & PIPERADE TARTINE

SERVES 4

4 thick slices sourdough bread

extra virgin olive oil, for brushing and drizzling

2 garlic cloves, cut in half

75 g anchovies in oil, drained

1 punnet baby basil, leaves picked, or a handful of small basil leaves

freshly ground black pepper

PIPERADE

2 tablespoons extra virgin olive oil

1 small onion, thinly sliced

5 garlic cloves, thinly sliced

1 teaspoon salted capers, rinsed and patted dry

1 red capsicum (pepper), membrane and seeds removed, cut into 5 mm strips

1 green capsicum (pepper), membrane and seeds removed, cut into 5 mm strips

1 yellow capsicum (pepper), membrane and seeds removed, cut into 5 mm strips

125 ml (½ cup) white wine

6 cherry tomatoes

small handful of basil leaves, chopped

small handful of flat-leaf parsley leaves, chopped

salt flakes and freshly ground black pepper

a little red wine vinegar or balsamic vinegar (optional)

A classic dish of braised capsicums with tomatoes and onions from the Basque Country, piperade captures the colours of the Basque flag (red, green and white). Piled on toast and paired with the saltiness of anchovies, this is heaven. Buy the best anchovies you can find, as the simplicity of this dish demands quality ingredients. To make it a little more substantial, serve a poached or fried egg on top.

For the piperade, warm the olive oil in a frying pan over low heat and sweat the onion, garlic and capers until the onion is soft and translucent. Add the capsicums and wine and simmer until the liquid is reduced to a syrupy glaze. Add the tomatoes and stew slowly to make a thick sauce, about 30 minutes. Add the chopped basil and parsley, then remove from the heat and season to taste with salt and pepper. If you find it a little sweet, add a dash of red wine vinegar or balsamic. Leave to cool to room temperature.

Heat a barbecue or chargrill pan to hot. Brush the slices of bread with olive oil, then grill on both sides.

When the bread is toasted, rub with the cut cloves of garlic, then spoon on the piperade, drizzling over some of the beautiful red oil. Top with the anchovies, then scatter over the basil. Finish with a grinding of pepper and a drizzle of olive oil.

130

BAKED FLATHEAD WITH BRAISED WHITE BEANS & ROMESCO SAUCE

SERVES 4

1 × 1.2 kg or 4 × 400 g flathead, scaled and gutted, fins removed

salt flakes and freshly ground black pepper

240 g lardo or pancetta, thinly sliced

60 ml (¼ cup) extra virgin olive oil

½ bunch chives, cut into 4 cm lengths

1 lemon, cut into wedges

romesco sauce (see page 237), to serve

BRAISED WHITE BEANS

125 g great northern beans or cannellini beans

pinch of bicarbonate of soda

1 tablespoon duck fat or olive oil

80 g piquillo peppers, cut into strips

½ small onion, diced

1 small carrot, diced

1 teaspoon smoked sweet paprika

100 ml white wine

pinch of saffron threads

about 500 ml (2 cups) chicken stock (see page 241)

4 thyme sprigs

2 bay leaves

5 garlic cloves, crushed

handful of flat-leaf parsley leaves, chopped

salt flakes and freshly ground white pepper

handful of baby spinach leaves

handful of dill fronds, chopped

This recipe can be made with one large fish or four smaller ones, and if flathead isn't available, rock cod, bar cod or rockling would also work well. Piquillo peppers are available in jars from specialist food shops, and terracotta roof tiles can be found in most hardware stores – I got mine from the local tiling shop. Just make sure they are pure terracotta (glazed or unglazed), rather than concrete or cement. Before using the tiles, wash them well and leave to soak in water overnight, so they won't crack when exposed to heat. Remember to soak the beans overnight too.

If the weather cooperates, you can cook the fish on the barbecue over hot coals – this way you'll get the most benefit from cooking the fish on roof tiles. Just keep an eye on it, as the lardo will melt and can cause flare-ups.

For the braised white beans, soak the beans overnight in 1 litre (4 cups) of water with the bicarbonate of soda.

The next day, drain the beans and rinse well, then place in a saucepan, cover with fresh water and bring to the boil. Reduce the heat and simmer for 10 minutes, then drain and rinse again.

Heat the duck fat or olive oil in a flameproof casserole with a lid over medium heat, add the pepper strips, onion and carrot and saute until lightly coloured. Add the paprika and stir for 30 seconds, then add the wine and saffron and simmer until reduced by half.

Add the beans and top up with enough stock to cover by 2 cm. Add the thyme and bay leaves and simmer, covered, for 2 hours or until the beans are tender, adding more stock as needed. Stir in the garlic and parsley and season to taste with salt and pepper. Fold through the spinach and dill, then leave to stand for 20 minutes.

About 30 minutes before the beans will be ready, preheat the oven to 220°C.

Season the fish with salt and pepper. Wrap with overlapping slices of lardo or pancetta, then carefully transfer to a terracotta roof tile or a good solid baking tray and drizzle with olive oil. If cooking the fish on a roof tile, place the tile on a baking tray to catch any drips. Bake for about 10–15 minutes or until just cooked through. Check by gently pressing the fish – the flesh should yield under the pressure of your finger.

When the fish is done, remove it from the oven and allow to sit for 5 minutes (the terracotta tile will be very hot, so be careful).

Scatter the fish with chives and place in the centre of the table with lemon wedges for squeezing. Serve with the beans and romesco sauce on the side.

BRAISED SKATE WITH RED WINE & LENTILS

SERVES 4

200 g puy-style lentils

1 tablespoon olive oil

1 carrot, cut into 1 cm dice

1 small onion, cut into 1 cm dice

1 small celery stick, cut into
1 cm dice

5 garlic cloves, thinly sliced

75 g bacon, cut into 1 cm dice

1 bay leaf

1 teaspoon thyme leaves

125 ml (½ cup) white wine

750 ml (3 cups) chicken stock
(see page 241)

60 g butter

salt flakes and freshly ground
black pepper

1 × 1.2 kg piece skate wing

plain flour, for dusting

250 ml (1 cup) red wine

125 g red wine butter
(see page 227)

small handful of flat-leaf parsley
leaves, finely shredded

If you have trouble finding skate, flounder makes a nice alternative. As this red wine butter will keep for up to a month in the fridge or 3 months in the freezer, and a slice of it will add richness and flavour to any simply cooked fish or a steak, you might want to make a double batch.

Place the lentils in a saucepan, cover with cold water and bring to the boil, then drain in a sieve and rinse well.

Wipe the pan dry, then add the olive oil and place over medium heat. Add the carrot, onion, celery, garlic, bacon, bay leaf and thyme and saute until the bacon has rendered its fat and the vegetables are lightly coloured. Add the white wine and simmer until reduced to a syrup-like glaze. Stir in the lentils, then pour in 500 ml (2 cups) of the stock and simmer for about 45 minutes until the lentils are tender. Fold in 20 g of the butter, then remove from the heat and season to taste with salt and pepper.

Melt the remaining butter in a large frying pan over medium–high heat. Dust the skate in seasoned flour, then carefully lower into the pan and fry for 5 minutes on each side in the foaming butter until golden. Add the red wine and the remaining 250 ml (1 cup) of stock and simmer for 3 minutes, then carefully turn the fish and simmer for another 3 minutes. Remove from the heat and allow the fish to rest in the pan for 2 minutes.

Tip the lentils into a warmed serving dish. Place the skate on top, reserving the juices in the frying pan. Cut half of the red wine butter into discs and place on the skate, then scatter with the shredded parsley.

Add the remaining red wine butter to the cooking juices in the frying pan and place over medium heat. When the butter has melted and the sauce has emulsified, pour into a warmed jug and serve alongside the skate and lentils.

134

GRILLED SARDINES IN VINE LEAVES

SERVES 4

12 fresh or preserved vine leaves, rinsed

12 sardines, scaled and gutted

1 preserved lemon quarter, rind only, finely diced

2 tablespoons pine nuts, lightly toasted

2 teaspoons salted capers, soaked, rinsed and patted dry

small handful of mint leaves, roughly chopped

small handful of flat-leaf parsley leaves, roughly chopped

small handful of dill leaves, roughly chopped

60 g raisins, chopped

60 ml (¼ cup) extra virgin olive oil, plus extra for brushing

salt flakes

LEMON & OLIVE OIL DRESSING

80 ml (⅓ cup) extra virgin olive oil

finely grated zest and juice of ½ lemon

salt flakes and freshly ground white pepper

I love sardines. They are so underrated, yet pack such a punch of flavour. If you can't find whole sardines at the market, then trunks (no head or tail) or butterflied fillets (no head, no tail, no bones) are the next best things. While you are on your shopping travels, if you find any dried raisins on the vine, snap them up – they tend to be larger and sweeter, with a lovely firm texture. Buy extra to serve with cheese, for tossing through salads or to make the raisin water for your sourdough starter (see page 202).

To ring the changes, you could serve these sardines with the harissa on page 233 or the roman beans on page 82.

To make the dressing, whisk together the olive oil and lemon juice and zest in a small bowl and season to taste with salt and pepper.

If using fresh vine leaves, plunge them in lightly salted boiling water for 30 seconds, then remove and cool in a bowl of iced water. Drain on a clean cloth or paper towel. If using preserved vine leaves, give them a good rinse, then pat dry with paper towel. Remove the stalk from the leaves.

Snip the sardine backbones at both ends of the cavity and remove the ribs – they should lift out very easily.

Combine the remaining ingredients except the salt and stuff the sardine cavities with this mixture, then season with a little salt. Roll each sardine in a damp vine leaf to make a neat parcel.

Heat a barbecue grillplate or chargrill pan over high heat. Brush the sardine parcels with a little olive oil, then grill for 1–2 minutes each side or until cooked through.

Spoon the dressing over the sardines and serve warm.

CASSOULET WITH DUCK CONFIT

SERVES 6
(OR 4 GREEDY PEOPLE)

250 g dried tarbais or great
   northern beans

pinch of bicarbonate of soda

25 g duck fat

400 g pork belly, bone in, skin on

2 Toulouse sausages

2 unsmoked ham hocks

175 ml white wine

125 g tomatoes, diced

about 1 litre (4 cups) veal stock
   (see page 243) or water

20 garlic cloves, crushed

1 tablespoon thyme leaves

2 bay leaves

1 onion, diced

1 large carrot, diced

60 g pork back fat, minced

salt flakes and freshly ground
   white pepper

3 confit duck legs (see page 32)

150 g coarse breadcrumbs,
   preferably sourdough

large handful of flat-leaf parsley
   leaves, chopped

green salad, to serve

Cassoulet is a real show-stopper: a feast of tender meats cooked with white beans, it is truly a work of art. Your butcher should have pork back fat and Toulouse sausages; however it is a good idea to order all the meat you'll need for this in advance to avoid disappointment.

Soak the beans overnight in 1 litre (4 cups) water with a pinch of bicarbonate of soda. The next day, drain the beans and rinse well, then place in a saucepan, cover with fresh water and bring to the boil. Reduce the heat and simmer for 10 minutes, then drain and rinse again.

Heat the duck fat in a large heavy-based saucepan and brown the pork belly. Remove from the pan and repeat with the sausages, then the ham hocks. Carefully pour the fat from the pan into a bowl and reserve. Deglaze the pan with the wine and simmer until it has reduced by half. Return the browned pork belly, sausages and ham hocks to the pan, add the tomato and pour in enough stock or water to cover. Bring to the boil, then reduce the heat to a simmer. Add three-quarters of the garlic, plus the thyme and bay leaves and simmer gently for 45 minutes. Remove the sausages and continue simmering for another 1¼ hours.

In a small frying pan, heat the reserved fat from browning the meats and saute the onion and carrot until softened. Add to the saucepan, along with the beans, pork back fat and the remaining garlic and simmer for 1 hour or until the beans are tender. Season to taste, then remove the pork belly and ham hocks and set aside to cool. Peel and thickly slice the sausages on the diagonal, cut the pork belly into thick slices and strip the ham from the hocks, discarding the skin and bones.

Preheat the oven to 160°C. Remove the skin from the confit duck legs and roast for 20 minutes. Drain the crisped skin on paper towel, reserving the rendered duck fat. Remove the duck meat from the bones.

Place half of the beans in the base of an earthenware or enamelled cast-iron casserole. Top with the pork, sausage, ham and duck meat, followed by the remaining beans, and bake for 30 minutes.

Meanwhile, melt the reserved duck fat in a frying pan and fry the breadcrumbs until crispy, then drain on paper towel.

Scatter the breadcrumbs over the cassoulet and let it sit for 10 minutes before sprinkling over the chopped parsley and serving. Crumble the crisp duck skin over a green salad and serve alongside the cassoulet.

136

BRAISED TRIPE WITH TOMATOES, MINT & PECORINO

SERVES 4

500 g honeycomb beef tripe
80 ml (⅓ cup) olive oil, plus
   extra for brushing
1 onion, diced
1 carrot, diced
½ fennel bulb, diced
6 garlic cloves, 5 thinly sliced,
   1 halved
salt flakes
1 tablespoon oregano leaves,
   chopped
1 tablespoon thyme leaves, chopped
1 bay leaf
125 ml (½ cup) white wine
4 ripe tomatoes, peeled, seeded
   and diced
20 g (¼ cup) grated parmesan
40 g (½ cup) grated pecorino
handful of mint leaves, shredded
juice of ½ lemon
large handful of rocket leaves
2 tablespoons extra virgin olive oil
4 thick slices sourdough bread

STOCK

60 ml (¼ cup) white wine
60 ml (¼ cup) white wine vinegar
½ leek, chopped
1 carrot, roughly chopped
2 sticks celery, roughly chopped
5 garlic cloves, halved
pinch of salt flakes
½ teaspoon white peppercorns
2 bay leaves
a few parsley stalks
a few sprigs of thyme
1 tablespoon olive oil
½ lemon

Many moons ago, Neil Perry and I cooked this to go on the menu at Star Grill, and it has remained a favourite of mine ever since. The rich, jammy texture and sweet, salty flavours make this a wonderful introduction for those trying tripe for the first time. You'll need to order the tripe in advance from your butcher – honeycomb is best for this recipe. And if you are a tripe novice, I suggest you ask for bleached tripe, as the strong flavour of unbleached tripe is something of an acquired taste.

For a heartier meal, you can add some cooked chickpeas and sliced potatoes to the braise, or serve it with pasta, but I find it hard to beat the simplicity of a rocket salad and toast.

Place all the stock ingredients except the lemon in a saucepan with 1 litre (4 cups) of water and bring to the boil. Simmer for 5 minutes, then remove from the heat. Add the lemon and leave the stock to cool to room temperature before straining through a fine-meshed sieve into a clean saucepan.

Wash the tripe then add to the pan of stock and simmer until tender, about 1 hour. Remove and cut into finger-sized strips and allow to cool.

In a heavy-based saucepan, heat 3 tablespoons of the olive oil over medium heat and saute the onion, carrot, fennel and sliced garlic with a pinch of salt until lightly browned. Add the oregano, thyme, bay leaf and wine and simmer until the liquid is reduced to a syrupy glaze. Add the diced tomatoes and cook until they break up, about 5 minutes.

Add the tripe and the remaining tablespoon of olive oil and continue cooking until the sauce begins to fry. Add the parmesan and pecorino and stir constantly until the cheeses have melted and the sauce has a jammy consistency. Remove from the heat, sprinkle over the mint and add a squeeze of lemon juice if the sauce tastes a little flat (the pecorino should have contributed enough saltiness).

Toss the rocket leaves the extra virgin olive oil and the remaining lemon juice. Brush the bread with extra olive oil and grill on a barbecue or chargrill pan, then rub with the cut side of the halved garlic clove.

Serve the tripe on plates with the grilled bread and rocket on the side.

GRILLED SQUAB, RADICCHIO, GRAPE & VINCOTTO SALAD

SERVES 4

125 ml (½ cup) extra virgin
  olive oil

80 ml (⅓ cup) vincotto

4 squab, butterflied

2 red capsicums (peppers)

1 head radicchio, leaves separated

120 g black grapes, halved
  and seeded

handful of walnuts, toasted

handful of mint leaves

chilli salt (see page 228) and
  freshly ground white pepper,
  to taste

This is an easy dish to cook on the barbecue while chatting to friends.

You'll probably need to order the squab from your butcher in advance – ask them to clean and prepare them for you by removing the backbone, wishbone, wing tips and gizzards, then butterflying the birds.

To shake things up a little, try making this with pomegranate instead of grapes and pomegranate molasses instead of vincotto. The walnuts add textural interest, but are not essential – feel free to leave them out if you have a nut allergy.

Combine 2 tablespoons of the olive oil and 2 tablespoons of the vincotto in a bowl. Add the squab, toss gently and leave to marinate for 45 minutes.

Meanwhile, preheat a barbecue or chargrill pan to hot.

Grill the capsicums to blacken their skins, then place in a sealed plastic bag and leave to sweat. When they are cool enough to handle, rub off the skins and remove the seeds, then cut the capsicum flesh into finger-sized strips.

Take the squab from the marinade and grill for about 5 minutes on each side (for medium-rare). Remove the squab from the grill and leave to rest for 5 minutes, then cut in half.

In a large bowl, combine the radicchio leaves, grapes, capsicum strips and walnuts with the remaining olive oil and vincotto. Toss gently, then transfer to a platter and arrange the squab on top. Pour the rest of the dressing from the bowl over the squab. Scatter the mint leaves over the salad and season to taste with chilli salt and pepper, then serve immediately.

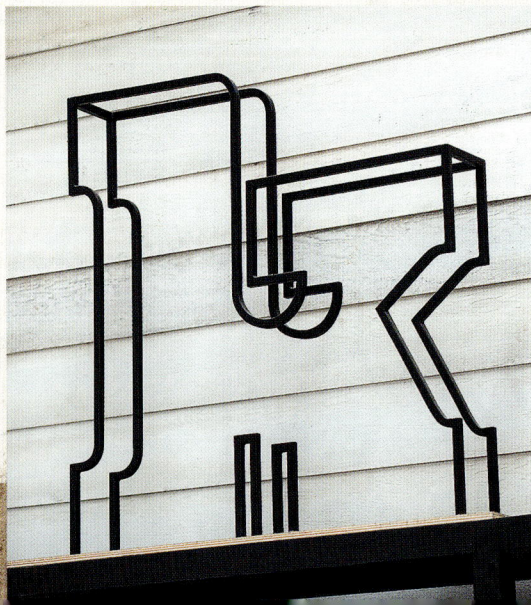

SERVES 4

200 ml chicken stock
(see page 241)

6 golden shallots, peeled

1 leek, white part only

1 large carrot, peeled or 1 bunch
baby carrots, trimmed

1 swede, peeled

10 garlic cloves, peeled

2 tablespoons olive oil

4 lamb neck chops

2 bay leaves

1 tablespoon thyme leaves

small handful of flat-leaf parsley
leaves, finely shredded

PEASE PUDDING

200 g dried yellow split peas

pinch of bicarbonate of soda

small handful of mint leaves,
chopped

1 smoked ham hock

This is my version of a soup from south-west Wales that dates back to the fourteenth century. The Welsh affinity with lamb and leeks is well known, and in many households, a soup like this would traditionally have been kept ticking away in the Aga or range cooker right through the chillier months. I've taken geographical liberties with the pease pudding, however, as this is more closely associated with the north-east of England. The 'pease pudding hot, pease pudding cold' of nursery rhyme fame, it's made from soaked split peas cooked in ham stock, and has the most wonderful texture and an earthy smokiness that offsets the soup beautifully.

For the pease pudding, soak the split peas overnight in 1 litre (4 cups) of water with the bicarbonate of soda.

The next day, grease and lightly flour a square of muslin. Drain and rinse the split peas, then combine with the mint and place in the centre of the muslin. Tie the four corners of the muslin securely with kitchen string, leaving plenty of room for the peas to swell as they cook. Lower the bundle into a large saucepan of water with the ham hock and simmer gently for 4 hours or until the ham is falling off the bone and the split peas are tender but still firm.

About 1½ hours before the pease pudding will be ready, preheat the oven to 140°C.

Pour the stock and 200 ml of water into a large saucepan and bring to the boil. Add the shallots, leek, carrot, swede and garlic and simmer slowly until tender. Remove each vegetable as it is cooked: test for doneness by piercing with a skewer – it should slide in easily. When all the vegetables are cooked, reserve the stock and allow the vegetables to cool, then cut into wedges and slices or whatever shape you like.

Heat the olive oil in a flameproof casserole with a lid over medium heat and sear the chops on both sides. Add the reserved stock from the vegetables, along with the bay leaves and thyme, then cover with the lid and braise in the oven for 1 hour or until the lamb is tender. Add the vegetables and return to the oven for another 5 minutes, just to heat the vegetables through and allow the flavours to mingle.

Remove the cawl from the oven and flake the ham into it, then scatter with parsley and place in the middle of the table. Carefully transfer the bundle of pease pudding from the pan to a bowl, untie and serve with the cawl.

142

CRISPY PORK BELLY WITH MANGO CHUTNEY

SERVES 4

160 g fine salt

2 kg pork belly on the bone, with skin

25 ml white wine

¼ bunch thyme

2 bay leaves

3 garlic cloves, peeled

1 litre (4 cups) vegetable oil

250 ml (1 cup) olive oil

salt flakes

mango chutney (see page 219), to serve

Start this recipe two days in advance, to allow time for brining, slow-cooking and pressing the pork before its final roasting. When you remove the bones from the slow-cooked pork, pick the meat from the bones and save this delicious pulled pork for a roll with slaw (see page 145).

Make a brine by dissolving the 160 g salt in 2 litres of cold water. Place the pork belly in a non-reactive container that will hold it snugly and pour over the brine. Leave to soak overnight in the refrigerator – you may need to weigh down the meat with a plate or similar to keep it submerged.

The next day, preheat the oven to 80°C. Remove the pork from the brine, pat it dry and lay it, skin-side down, in a roasting tin lined with baking paper. Add the wine, herbs, garlic, vegetable oil and olive oil, then cover with a lid or foil and cook in the oven for 10 hours. Because ovens can be very inconsistent at low temperatures, it's worth checking every now and then to make sure the oil isn't bubbling and the meat isn't exposed. After the 10 hours is up, carefully lift the pork belly out of the oil and place, skin-side down, on a baking tray lined with baking paper. Check to see if it's done: the bones should slip very easily out of joint; if they don't, put the pork belly back in the oil, increase the oven temperature to 90°C and return the pork to the oven until the meat loosens from the bones.

When the pork is ready, remove the bones (picking any meat from them for a sandwich – see page 145) and give the pork belly a light trim to remove any blood vessels and cartilage. Cover the meat with another sheet of baking paper and place another tray or plate on top, then weight with some tins of tomatoes or similar and refrigerate overnight to press and firm the pork belly.

Preheat the oven to 210°C and double-line a baking dish large enough to hold the pork belly with foil then baking paper. Using a sharp knife, score the pork skin in a 1 cm lattice pattern without going too far into the fat. Rub the skin with a couple of pinches of salt flakes and place the belly, skin-side up, in the prepared dish. Gather up the sides of the baking paper and foil around the pork and pour in enough water to come half-way up the belly – this keeps the flesh moist during cooking, yet allows the crackling to go crisp. Roast for 30–40 minutes until the skin is golden, then increase the oven temperature to 250°C to blister and finish the pork crackling. Remove the pork from the oven and leave to rest in the dish for 10 minutes before transferring to a board or platter and carving.

Place the pork in the centre of the table with a bowl of the chutney alongside, so people can help themselves.

PULLED PORK, SLAW & QUINCE ROLL

SERVES 4

4 sourdough bread rolls

butter, for spreading

160 g pulled pork

salt flakes and freshly ground
   black pepper

4 tablespoons quince relish (see
   page 222) or quince paste

4 sprigs watercress

CABBAGE, APPLE & WALNUT SLAW

¼ white cabbage, shredded

¼ red cabbage, shredded

½ small granny smith apple,
   thinly sliced

50 g (½ cup) walnuts, lightly
   toasted and roughly chopped

small handful of mint leaves

small handful of wild rocket leaves

2 tablespoons buttermilk

2 tablespoons extra virgin olive oil

1 tablespoon wholegrain mustard

salt flakes and freshly ground
   black pepper

This recipe makes good use of the luscious strands of meat picked from the bones of the pork belly in the recipe on page 142. Try to source real buttermilk (such as that made by Pepe Saya in New South Wales and Myrtleford Butter Factory in Victoria) for the slaw. You'll find the taste is fresher and more acidic and the texture is more viscous, which helps the dressing to coat the cabbage.

To make the slaw, place the cabbage, apple, walnuts, mint and rocket in a large bowl and toss gently together. In a small bowl, whisk together the buttermilk, olive oil and mustard to make a dressing. Season to taste with salt and pepper, then add the dressing to the slaw and toss again.

Split the rolls and spread with butter.

Season the pork with salt and pepper, then divide among the rolls. Place a small mound of slaw on top of the pork, then a spoonful of relish and a sprig of watercress for colour.

Close the roll and enjoy.

146

QUINCE WITH SAFFRON CUSTARD & PISTACHIO BRITTLE

SERVES 4

4 quinces
juice of ½ lemon
450 g caster sugar
1 vanilla bean
1 cinnamon quill
5 cloves
3 star anise
5 white peppercorns

PISTACHIO BRITTLE

210 g (1½ cups) unsalted pistachios, toasted under the grill
330 g (1½ cups) caster sugar
90 g (¼ cup) golden syrup
40 g butter
½ teaspoon bicarbonate of soda
¼ teaspoon salt flakes

SAFFRON CUSTARD

200 ml double cream
pinch of saffron threads
4 egg yolks
40 g caster sugar
1 teaspoon cornflour
pinch of freshly grated nutmeg

To really bring out their rosy hue and heady fragrance, the quince are slow-cooked for 12 hours (overnight works well). Given this lengthy cooking time, you might want to make a double batch of baked quince – they will keep for several weeks in the fridge and are lovely with breakfast muesli and yoghurt or alongside various desserts. The leftover pistachio brittle, which can be stored for 1 month in the freezer, is also useful to have on hand to perk up ice cream and other desserts. But if you don't have time to make the pistachio brittle, just sprinkle over some roughly chopped pistachios.

Wash and peel the quinces, keeping the skin. Cut each quince into quarters and core, reserving the cores as well. Place the quince quarters in a bowl of water with the lemon juice added, to stop them going brown. Put the sugar, all the spices and 1.25 litres (5 cups) of water into a saucepan. Add the reserved quince peelings and cores and bring to the boil, then simmer for 30 minutes.

Preheat the oven to 100°C. Drain the quince quarters, then place in a deep baking dish and cover with a layer of muslin. Pour in the syrup, including the peelings and cores and spices, spreading them over the muslin, then cover the baking dish tightly with a double layer of foil. Bake for 12 hours or until the quince is deep red and tender. When cool enough to handle, pull together the corners of the muslin, lifting away the quince cores and peelings and the spices, then discard.

To make the pistachio brittle, line a baking tray with baking paper and place on a wire rack, then scatter the pistachios evenly over the baking paper. Place the sugar, golden syrup, butter and 125 ml (½ cup) of water in a heavy-based saucepan over low–medium heat. Stir to dissolve the sugar, then simmer for 5 minutes, without stirring, until the caramel is a deep golden brown. Remove from the heat and whisk in the bicarbonate of soda and salt, then carefully pour over the pistachios on the prepared tray. Leave to cool until rock hard, then break into shards.

For the saffron custard, place the cream and saffron in a small saucepan and bring to the boil. Remove from the heat and allow to cool until it is lukewarm. In a heatproof bowl, whisk the egg yolks, sugar and cornflour together, then gently whisk in the warm saffron-infused cream. Set the bowl over a pan of gently simmering water and heat, stirring constantly, until the custard is thick enough to coat the back of the spoon. Do not allow the custard to boil or it will curdle. When the custard is ready, immediately remove the bowl from the heat and place in a sink full of cold water to stop the cooking process. Add freshly grated nutmeg to taste.

Serve the quince on a serving platter or in individual bowls with the saffron custard and pistachio brittle.

CHOCOLATE & WALNUT BROWNIES

MAKES ABOUT 12

5 eggs

400 g brown sugar

¼ teaspoon salt flakes

2 teaspoons vanilla extract

170 g butter

500 g dark chocolate (70% cocoa), broken into chunks

140 g plain flour, sifted

300 g walnut halves

cocoa powder, for dusting (optional)

A killer brownie recipe is crucial in any kitchen. This one is a winner that never fails – and for those with nut allergies, it is equally good without the nuts. These brownies will keep for a week in an airtight container, though they never seem to last that long in our house!

For an extra treat, serve with a bowl of creme fraiche or chantilly cream (see page 55).

Preheat the oven to 175°C. Lightly grease a brownie tin (about 33 cm × 23 cm), then line it with baking paper, leaving some overhang all around to help lift the cooked brownies out of the tin.

Place the eggs, sugar, salt and vanilla in the bowl of an electric mixer and whisk on high speed until the sugar has dissolved and the mixture is pale and doubled in volume.

Melt the butter in a saucepan, then remove from the heat and stir in the chocolate to melt. With the mixer running on low speed, slowly pour in the warm chocolate mixture to incorporate.

Remove the bowl from the mixer and gently fold in the sifted flour by hand, using a spatula and taking care not to knock the air out of the mixture.

Pour the brownie mixture into the prepared tin, smoothing the surface with your spatula. Drop the nuts onto the surface, allowing them to sink a little.

Bake for 25–30 minutes or until the top is glossy and cracked. The brownies will be soft to the touch, but will firm up as they cool – they should stay fudgy in the middle.

Leave to cool in the tin, then carefully remove and dust with cocoa, if desired, before cutting into squares.

FLOURLESS PISTACHIO CAKE

MAKES 1 × 20 CM CAKE

280 g (2 cups) unsalted
  pistachios, lightly toasted
6 eggs, separated
185 g natural yoghurt
125 ml (½ cup) olive oil
1 teaspoon ground cardamom
finely grated zest of 1 orange
1 teaspoon rosewater
1 teaspoon vanilla extract
¾ teaspoon bicarbonate of soda
¼ teaspoon baking powder
220 g (1 cup) caster sugar
pure icing sugar, for dusting
thick cream, to serve

The ground pistachios give this cake its elegant pastel-green colour, and the egg whites give it a light, airy texture. It is especially delicious split and filled with creme patissiere (see page 102), then drizzled with honey.

When you have time on your hands, make two of these cakes then wrap one in cling film and foil and keep in the freezer for another time – it will only take half an hour to thaw.

Preheat the oven to 180°C. Line a round 20 cm cake tin with baking paper.

Finely grind the pistachios in a food processor.

Place the egg yolks, yoghurt, olive oil, cardamom, orange zest, rosewater, vanilla, bicarbonate of soda, baking powder and half of the sugar in the bowl of an electric mixer and whisk until pale and doubled in volume. Transfer to a large bowl and gently fold in the ground pistachios by hand, using a spatula and taking care not to knock the air out of the mixture.

In the thoroughly washed and dried bowl of your electric mixer, whisk the egg whites to soft peaks. Add the remaining sugar and keep whisking until glossy stiff peaks form.

Gently fold the egg white mixture into the batter with your spatula, again being careful to knock out as little air as possible.

Pour into the prepared tin and bake for 1 hour or until a skewer inserted in the centre comes out clean.

Leave the cake to cool in its tin on a wire rack, then carefully remove from the tin.

Dust with icing sugar and serve with thick cream.

RHUBARB TRIFLE

SERVES 8

900 g rhubarb

90 g caster sugar

3 titanium-strength gelatine leaves

80 ml (⅓ cup) ginger wine

160 g savoiardi biscuits

unsalted pistachios or pistachio brittle (see page 146), to serve

RHUBARB COMPOTE

600 g rhubarb, cut into 4 cm lengths

180 g caster sugar

juice of 1 lemon

VANILLA CUSTARD

700 ml milk

2 vanilla beans, split and seeds scraped

6 egg yolks

140 g caster sugar

80 g cornflour

200 ml double cream

Start this recipe ahead of time, as the rhubarb for the compote needs to be steeped overnight and the jelly needs time to set. The finished trifle is always better the day after it is made, when all of the flavours have come together. For a more traditional trifle, use sherry instead of ginger wine.

Ideally, you need a juicer to juice the rhubarb for this dessert. If you don't have one, blend the rhubarb with the sugar for the jelly in a blender until smooth, then pass the juice through a muslin-lined sieve to catch any stringy bits before warming in a saucepan and adding the gelatine.

For the compote, toss the rhubarb with the sugar in a non-reactive saucepan. Cover and leave to steep overnight at room temperature. The next day, bring to the boil, then cover and remove from the heat. Let the residual heat cook the rhubarb through. When it is tender, store it in the fridge.

Juice the 900 g rhubarb – you should get about 400 ml juice. Pour 320 ml of the rhubarb juice into a small non-reactive saucepan. Add the sugar, then place over medium heat and simmer until the sugar has dissolved. Soften the gelatine in cold water for 5 minutes, then squeeze out and add to the pan. Stir until completely dissolved before straining into a rectangular tray or dish. Refrigerate for 2 hours or until set into a jelly, then cut into cubes.

To make the custard, place half of the milk and the vanilla seeds in a small saucepan and bring to the boil. Remove from the heat and leave to infuse for 15 minutes.

Meanwhile, in another bowl, whisk the egg yolks and sugar until light and fluffy. Whisk in the cornflour until there are no lumps, then whisk in the remaining milk until smooth.

Pour the egg yolk mixture into the pan of warm infused milk and place over low–medium heat. Bring to the boil slowly, stirring constantly, until thick enough to coat the back of the spoon. Remove from the heat and let the custard cool to room temperature before folding in the cream.

When you're ready to assemble the trifle, combine the remaining rhubarb juice with the ginger wine. Place a layer of jelly cubes in the base of a large glass bowl or individual glasses, then place a layer of savoiardi biscuits on top and drizzle with the rhubarb juice and ginger wine. Cover with a layer of custard, then spoon over the compote. Repeat until all the ingredients are used up, then scatter with pistachios or crumbled pistachio brittle and serve.

SERVES 4—6

12 tamarillos

300 ml port

400 ml verjus

330 g (1½ cups) caster sugar

5 green cardamom pods

2 cinnamon quills

5 cloves

3 cm knob ginger, half thinly sliced and half cut into fine matchsticks

Start this recipe the day before, as the tamarillos are left to cool in their poaching liquid overnight and absorb all the flavours. You can use the leftover poaching liquid to make a granita. Just mix with an equal volume of port (or Aperol or Campari, if you prefer) and freeze in a shallow dish or tray for at least 3 hours, scraping the ice crystals with a fork every 30 minutes, until you have a flaky granita.

These tamarillos make a lovely addition to a weekend brunch. Serve with a bowl of mascarpone and brioche (see page 208) for an extra treat. If you develop a taste for them, make a double batch and bottle them while they're still hot in a sterilised jar (see page 224). Unopened, they will keep in a cool, dark place for up to a month. Refrigerate once the jar is open and use within 2 weeks.

Put the tamarillos, port, verjus, sugar, cardamom, cinnamon, cloves and ginger slices into a non-reactive saucepan. Place a circle of baking paper on the surface of the liquid to keep the tamarillos from drying out as they cook.

Bring to the boil, then cover with a lid and simmer slowly until the tamarillos are just tender, about 20 minutes. Leave the tamarillos to cool in the liquid overnight in the fridge.

The next day, use a slotted spoon to transfer the tamarillos to a serving plate.

Strain the poaching liquid and measure out 375 ml (1½ cups) into a small saucepan (the rest of the liquid can be made into a granita – see above). Add the ginger matchsticks and simmer over low heat until the liquid is reduced by half, about 10 minutes.

Pour the syrup and ginger matchsticks over the tamarillos and serve.

GRAPE & ROSEMARY BRIOCHE

SERVES 8–10

525 g (3½ cups) plain flour

75 g (⅓ cup) caster sugar,
plus 1 tablespoon extra

30 g dried yeast

5 eggs

115 ml full-cream milk

salt flakes

180 g butter, at room temperature

150 g seedless grapes, halved

handful of rosemary leaves

extra virgin olive oil, for drizzling

This is lovely for breakfast or afternoon tea – at its best served still warm from the oven, it doesn't need a thing. My biggest piece of advice for making the dough is to bring the butter to room temperature before adding it. This means the butter will be absorbed more quickly, which reduces the risk of over-heating the dough by over-mixing it.

Sift the flour into the bowl of an electric mixer fitted with a dough hook, then stir in the sugar and yeast. In another bowl, whisk together the eggs, milk and a teaspoon of salt.

Turn the mixer on at low speed and slowly add the egg and milk mixture to the dry ingredients. When all of it has been incorporated, increase the speed to medium and keep mixing for 5 minutes longer or until the dough starts to come together.

Turn the speed up to medium–high and add the softened butter a teaspoon at a time, waiting until each addition has been fully incorporated before adding the next. Once all the butter has been added, keep mixing for 5 minutes longer or until the dough slaps the side of the bowl and comes away cleanly.

Cover the bowl with cling film and leave the dough in a warm place to prove until doubled in size, about 2 hours.

Knock back the dough, then cover the bowl again and refrigerate overnight until the dough has doubled in size.

Lightly grease a baking tray measuring about 33 cm × 23 cm, then line it with baking paper. Lay the brioche dough in the tray, gently stretching it to fit. Dimple the surface with your fingers, then scatter over the grapes and rosemary and sprinkle with a pinch of salt.

Leave to come to room temperature and prove until almost doubled in size again, about 1 hour.

Preheat the oven to 175°C.

Bake the brioche for 15–20 minutes until risen and deep golden brown, then remove from the oven. Dissolve the extra tablespoon of sugar in a tablespoon of boiling water and brush this syrup over the brioche to glaze. To serve, cut the brioche into squares and drizzle with olive oil.

WIN

CHAPTER 4

PORRIDGE WITH HONEYCOMB

SERVES 4

135 g (1½ cups) rolled oats
(not instant)
salt flakes
60 g honeycomb

I am a purist who really enjoys the simple nourishment of porridge, so I don't cook the oats with milk. I do like to serve the cooked porridge with a splash of cold milk, though, both to enrich it and to help bring the temperature down so you don't burn your mouth. To give your porridge the super-food edge, add 2 tablespoons of red quinoa to the oats when you start to cook them.

These days honeycomb is readily available from good food shops, but try to find one of the growing number of urban beekeepers who sell their honeycomb. They say that if you eat honey from your immediate area, you will never get sick. If you can't find honeycomb or even honey, try this with brown sugar – my little boys prefer it!

Combine the oats with 1.125 litres (4½ cups) of cold water in a saucepan and leave to sit for 30 minutes, or overnight if this works better with your schedule. Soaking the oats softens them and reduces their cooking time.

Place the pan over medium heat and bring to the boil. Add a pinch of salt, then turn down the heat and simmer slowly, stirring regularly, for about 10 minutes until the porridge is thick and creamy.

Remove from the heat, cover and leave to sit for 2 minutes.

Serve the porridge in individual bowls with a chunk of honeycomb on top.

GRATED BEETROOT, CARROT & FENNEL WITH ALFALFA & POACHED EGG

SERVES 4

1 large beetroot, peeled and grated

2 carrots, peeled and grated

1 large fennel bulb, grated

1 punnet alfalfa sprouts

½ bunch tarragon, leaves picked

½ bunch chives, finely sliced

½ bunch parsley, leaves picked and torn

½ bunch mint, leaves picked and torn

1 punnet baby coriander or a handful of regular coriander leaves

salt flakes and freshly ground black pepper

juice of ½ lemon

2 tablespoons extra virgin olive oil, plus extra for drizzling

2 teaspoons cumin seeds

4 tablespoons white quinoa

4 eggs

1–2 teaspoons vinegar

I feel so healthy when I eat this for breakfast. The raw vegetables and sprouts are not only good for you, but their contrasting textures with the creamy poached egg, boosted by the crunch of cumin seeds and quinoa, is a dream. For a final flourish, drizzle this earthy salad with some basil oil or chilli oil (see page 226).

Place the grated vegetables, alfalfa sprouts and all of the herbs except the coriander in a large bowl and toss together. Season with salt and pepper, then dress with lemon juice and olive oil.

Heat a heavy-based frying pan over medium heat and toast the cumin seeds until aromatic, then transfer to a mortar and coarsely crush with the pestle. Add the quinoa to the frying pan and toast until it smells nutty and starts to pop, then stir into the crushed cumin.

Bring a deep narrow pan of water to the boil (I find the deeper the pan, the better the poached egg, as the egg grows a tail as it cooks and assumes a lovely, ghost-like form), then add 1 teaspoon of vinegar and 2 teaspoons of salt per litre of water. Crack each egg into a cup. Turn the heat down so the water is just simmering, then stir the water in one direction to form a vortex. Slip the eggs, one at a time, into the vortex and allow to slowly circle down to the bottom of the pan. The eggs will float to the top when they are ready, about 2 minutes. A perfectly poached egg should feel like a balloon – soft but resilient. Remove from the pan and drain on paper towel.

Divide the grated vegetable and herb mixture among four bowls and place a warm poached egg on top of each one. Season the egg with salt, scatter with the toasted cumin and quinoa, then drizzle with a little extra olive oil and serve immediately.

ROAST BEETS WITH CHICKPEAS & GOAT'S CHEESE

SERVES 4

200 g large red beetroot

2 tablespoons olive oil

salt flakes and freshly ground black pepper

200 g golden beetroot

200 g baby red beetroot

200 g cooked chickpeas, drained

60 g baby chard leaves

4 tablespoons extra virgin olive oil, plus extra for drizzling

1 tablespoon red wine vinegar

100 g goat's curd or mild soft goat's cheese

Sunshine in a bowl for a cold winter's day. This simple salad is all about finding the very best ingredients, so don't worry if you can't get all three different kinds of beetroot — just use more of whatever you have. And if you fancy a change from chickpeas, try this with other pulses, such as black or green lentils, or with freekeh. A sprinkle of dukkah or sumac just before serving will give your salad a Middle Eastern touch.

Preheat the oven to 180°C.

Rub the large red beetroot with olive oil and season with salt and pepper, then wrap in a sheet of foil and place in the oven. Do the same with the golden and baby red beetroot. Roast all the beetroot until cooked through when tested with a skewer — about 1½ hours for the larger beets, 30 minutes less for the smaller ones. (If you have asbestos chef's fingers, another sign of doneness is that you can easily rub the skin off the beetroot with your fingers.) Leave the beets to cool, then peel and cut the larger beets into wedges and leave the baby beets whole.

Place all the beetroot in a large bowl. Add the chickpeas and chard and toss together. Season with salt and pepper, then dress with the extra virgin olive oil and vinegar and toss very well.

Crumble half of the goat's cheese into the bowl and toss lightly — the cheese will break up to enrich the salad and make the dressing bright purple.

Place the salad in a neat pile and crumble over the remaining goat's cheese. Drizzle with a little more olive oil and grind over some black pepper before serving.

SALAD OF BLOOD ORANGE CURED MACKEREL

SERVES 4

3 tablespoons white wine
3 tablespoons white wine vinegar
3 tablespoons caster sugar
pinch of salt
1 red witlof (chicory), leaves separated
1 white witlof (chicory), leaves separated
2 blood oranges, segmented
handful of dill sprigs
1 punnet celery cress, picked
100 ml pistachio oil (see page 227)

CURED MACKEREL

400 g blue mackerel fillet
juice of 2 blood oranges
2 red shallots, finely chopped
2 bird's eye chillies, chopped
1 fennel bulb, very finely sliced
1 teaspoon caster sugar
¼ teaspoon sweet paprika
1 tablespoon salt flakes
handful of dill, chopped

This is a great winter salad. It lends itself to being prepared the day before, so you just have to assemble it on the day – simply remove the fish from the curing liquid after 3 hours, wrap tightly in cling film and keep in the fridge until ready to use. Mackerel is perfect for this recipe, as it is lovely and oily, with a full flavour that will stand up to the boldness of the pickled witlof, citrus and pistachio oil.

For the cured mackerel, place all the ingredients in a non-reactive bowl and mix very well, then leave to cure in the fridge for 3 hours.

Meanwhile, place the white wine, vinegar, sugar, salt and 3 tablespoons of water in a large stainless-steel saucepan and bring to the boil, then remove from the heat. Plunge the witlof leaves into the pickling liquid, then set aside for at least 2 hours (or up to 24 hours).

Remove the mackerel from its curing liquid and pat dry. Reserve the fennel and the curing liquid.

Arrange the fennel, witlof and orange segments on a platter. Cut the fish into large chunks and add to the platter, then scatter with dill sprigs and celery cress. Mix about 3 tablespoons of the reserved curing liquid with the pistachio oil and drizzle over the salad. Serve immediately.

172 CHICKEN LIVER PARFAIT WITH WATERCRESS

SERVES 4

200 g chicken livers

250 ml (1 cup) milk

2 eggs

120 ml cream

1 tablespoon port

pinch of salt flakes

¼ teaspoon four-spice salt
(see page 228)

50 g butter, melted

watercress sprigs and toasted
brioche or sourdough, to serve

PORT & JUNIPER JELLY

250 ml (1 cup) port

10 juniper berries, bruised

125 ml (½ cup) chicken stock
(see page 241)

1¼ titanium-strength gelatine
leaves, soaked in cold water
to soften then squeezed out

MUSTARD & VERJUS
VINAIGRETTE

1 teaspoon Dijon mustard

½ teaspoon verjus

salt flakes and freshly ground
white pepper

1 teaspoon vegetable oil

2 teaspoons extra virgin olive oil

You'll need to start this 2 days ahead, as the chicken livers are steeped in milk overnight and then the parfait needs to set in the fridge the next night. If you don't have four 100 ml jars to make individual parfaits, this recipe works equally well in a terrine mould – you'll need to use three times the amounts given below to fill a 1-litre terrine mould, and increase the cooking time to approximately 35 minutes, or until the parfait is just set around the edges but still has a slight wobble in the centre. Sealing the parfait with the jelly means it will keep for longer (up to 10 days in the fridge) and won't discolour.

Pear & tomato chutney (see page 220) or quince relish (see page 222) both go beautifully with this. I also like to serve a small ramekin of four-spice salt (see page 228) alongside, in case people want to adjust the seasoning.

Trim the chicken livers of any connective tissue, then soak in the milk overnight in the fridge. The next day, drain the livers and pat dry, then leave to come to room temperature for about an hour. Remove the eggs and cream from the fridge and bring to room temperature. Blend the livers to a puree in a blender, then add the eggs, port, salt and four-spice salt and blend again until smooth. Finally, blend in the cream and the melted butter.

Preheat the oven to 140°C.

Pass the parfait mixure through muslin, wringing to extract as much as possible, then pour into four 100 ml jars or moulds.

Cover each jar or mould with foil, then place in a roasting tin and pour in hot water to come two-thirds of the way up the sides of the jars. Carefully transfer to the oven and cook for 10–15 minutes or until the parfait is barely set in the centre. Remove the jars from the water bath and leave to cool slightly, then place in the fridge for about 20 minutes.

Meanwhile, to make the jelly, place the port and juniper berries in a small pan and simmer until reduced by half. Add the stock and simmer until reduced to 125 ml (½ cup). Add the gelatine to the pan and stir over low heat until completely dissolved. Remove from the heat and set aside to cool slightly. When the jelly is tepid, pour a thin layer over each parfait, then chill until set, about 1 hour.

For the vinaigrette, whisk the mustard and vinegar together with a pinch of salt and a grinding of white pepper, then slowly drizzle in the oils, whisking constantly to emulsify into a thick dressing. Toss with the watercress sprigs.

Serve the parfaits in their jars or scoop onto plates with a hot spoon. Serve with toast and the dressed watercress.

TORN LAMB, ROCKET, MARINATED EGGPLANT & HARISSA MAYO WRAP

SERVES 4

4 tablespoons mayonnaise
(see page 235)

2 teaspoons harissa
(see page 233)

4 flatbread wraps

4 handfuls of rocket

400 g leftover slow-cooked lamb,
torn into chunks

MARINATED EGGPLANT

2 eggplants, cut lengthways
into 1 cm slices

small handful of marjoram leaves

large handful of coriander leaves

1 long red chilli, seeded and
chopped

2 garlic cloves, crushed

2 tablespoons extra virgin olive oil,
plus extra for brushing

juice of ½ lemon

salt flakes and freshly ground
black pepper

This is a great way of using up seven-hour pot-roast leg of lamb (see page 188), if you have any left over. The eggplant can be done a day or so in advance and kept in the fridge – it will only get better as it laps up the marinade. And if you're pressed for time, you could use good-quality readymade mayonnaise and harissa.

For the marinated eggplant, sprinkle the eggplant slices with a pinch of salt and set aside for 30 minutes.

Meanwhile, use a small food processor to blitz the marjoram, coriander, chilli, garlic, olive oil and lemon juice until smooth, adding salt and pepper to taste.

Drain the eggplant and pat dry. Brush with the extra olive oil and cook on a hot barbecue or chargrill pan until tender. Pour the marinade over the grilled eggplant and leave for at least 20 minutes before using.

Mix together the mayonnaise and harissa in a small bowl.

Lay a flatbread wrap on the benchtop and spread with the harissa mayonnaise. Arrange a quarter of the ingredients in a line down the centre. Fold in the ends, then roll into a fat cylinder and wrap tightly in greaseproof paper to hold it together.

Don't be tempted to toast the wraps or the mayo will split and become oily.

EGGY SILVERBEET & GRUYERE GRATIN

SERVES 4

500 ml (2 cups) cream

100 ml full-cream milk

2 garlic cloves, minced

1 tablespoon thyme leaves

1 kg silverbeet (Swiss chard),
   leave torn, stems finely chopped

3 eggs, beaten

120 g (1 cup) grated gruyere
   cheese

salt flakes and freshly ground
   black pepper

40 g (½ cup) grated parmesan

pinch of freshly grated nutmeg

This hearty gratin is full of flavour, without the heaviness of a flour-based sauce – the egg sets lightly in the oven, like a custard. This is perfect on a winter's night with a glass of red, or to accompany some simply cooked meat or fish.

Pour the cream and milk into a saucepan and add the garlic and thyme. Bring to the boil, then remove from the heat and set aside to infuse and cool.

Meanwhile, blanch the silverbeet in boiling water for about 2 minutes, just until wilted, then drain well.

Preheat the oven to 160°C.

When the cream mixture is tepid, whisk in the eggs and gruyere cheese and season with a pinch of salt and a grinding of pepper. Fold through the silverbeet, then transfer to a baking dish. Scatter with the parmesan and cook in the oven for 20 minutes or until just set.

Remove the gratin from the oven and leave to settle for 5 minutes. Sprinkle with nutmeg before serving.

178

WOOD-FIRED BROCCOLINI WITH LEMON & MARJORAM

SERVES 4

1 kg broccolini
60 ml (¼ cup) extra virgin olive oil
1 lemon, thinly sliced
large pinch of salt flakes
2 long red chillies, finely sliced
4 tablespoons pumpkin seeds
handful of marjoram leaves

I like the extra flavour a wood-fired oven gives these simply dressed greens, but of course a regular oven is fine too. Broccolini, rape, kale or any other winter greens are delicious cooked in this way.

Preheat the oven to 250°C.

In a large bowl, toss the broccolini with half of the olive oil, the salt and lemon slices, then tip everything into a roasting tin and roast for 2 minutes.

Add the chilli and roast for a further 5 minutes or until the tips of the broccolini are charred and the lemon slices have broken down.

Fold through the pumpkin seeds and marjoram and roast for another 2 minutes.

Serve drizzled with the remaining olive oil.

ROQUEFORT, PEAR & HONEYCOMB TARTINE

SERVES 4

4 thick slices sourdough bread

3 tablespoons extra virgin olive oil

225 g roquefort cheese

60 g honeycomb

1 teaspoon sherry vinegar

2 pears, ideally beurre bosc

large handful of mache leaves

handful of pale frisee leaves
(keep the outer green leaves
for a salad)

40 g walnuts, toasted and
roughly chopped

salt flakes and freshly ground
black pepper

1 punnet celery cress, picked, or a
few young celery leaves from the
heart of a bunch

Salty cheese and honeycomb is one of those matches made in heaven. If you can't get your hands on some roquefort, try this with an Australian blue cheese, ideally one that's slightly salty. You can also use nashi pears or apples instead of beurre bosc pears, and some runny honey if you don't have any honeycomb.

Brush the bread with 2 tablespoons of the olive oil and toast on the barbecue or under a hot grill.

Cut the cheese into thin wedges and lay over the slices of toast. Cut the honeycomb into four pieces and place on one end of each slice of toast.

Combine the remaining tablespoon of olive oil with the sherry vinegar to make a dressing.

Core and finely slice the pears, then cut into matchsticks. Place in a bowl with the mache, frisee and walnuts, then pour over the dressing and season with salt and pepper. Gently toss together.

Scatter the pear mixture over the cheese, avoiding the honeycomb. Garnish with celery cress or leaves, then serve with an extra grinding of pepper.

PIZZA MARGHERITA

MAKES 4 INDIVIDUAL PIZZAS OR 1 LARGE ONE FOR SHARING

1 kg sourdough bread dough (see page 205)

olive oil, for brushing

flour, for dusting

350 g buffalo mozzarella

basil leaves, salt flakes and extra virgin olive oil, to serve

TOMATO SAUCE

200 g canned tomatoes

3 garlic cloves, minced

10 ml extra virgin olive oil

pinch of salt flakes

handful of oregano leaves, chopped

small handful of basil leaves, chopped

Making pizza at home is an exciting thing, especially if you are blessed with a brick oven that can hit temperatures of 400°C plus! But don't be discouraged if you belong to the 99 per cent of people that don't have one – I've increased the water content of the pizza dough in this recipe, so your pizza will cook in a regular domestic oven without becoming dry and biscuity. Just remember to make the dough the day before, as it needs to rest overnight.

The other thing that helps to achieve good results is a pizza stone. Available from kitchenware shops and barbecue stores, this will help the pizza cook faster, producing a moist pizza with a crisp base.

If making individual pizzas, divide the dough into four balls. Brush a baking dish with olive oil and place the dough in the dish, brushing it with more oil to coat and leaving some space around each ball of dough. Cover the dish with cling film then leave to prove and rest in the fridge overnight.

For the tomato sauce, combine all the ingredients and blitz briefly with a stick blender to make a rustic sauce.

Preheat your oven with a pizza stone in it for 30 minutes on full blast.

Stretch the dough with the back of your hand, rotating it until it is thin in the middle and slightly thicker at the edges. For individual pizzas, shape each ball of dough into a round; for a large pizza to share, a slipper shape works well.

Dust the back of a large baking tray with flour and place the dough on the tray. Spread with the tomato sauce and top with torn pieces of mozzarella.

Open the oven door and carefully slide the pizza(s) off the tray and onto the pizza stone. Bake for about 5 minutes or until crisp. If you have a pizza oven that reaches a temperature of 350°C or more, your pizza will cook in less than 2 minutes.

Remove from the oven, scatter with basil leaves, season with a little salt and drizzle with olive oil, the serve immediately.

FISH PIE

SERVES 4

10 g butter

2 golden shallots, diced

1 teaspoon fennel seeds, lightly crushed

1 star anise, broken

300 ml vermouth

300 m fish stock (see page 242)

300 ml cream

280 g smoked mackerel fillet, skin removed, cut into 2 cm dice

280 g ocean trout fillet, skin removed, cut into 2 cm dice

280 g ling fillet, skin removed, cut into 2 cm dice

140 g frozen peas

4 hard-boiled eggs, peeled and cut into quarters

handful of flat-leaf parsley leaves, finely chopped

handful of dill, finely chopped

salt flakes and freshly ground white pepper

squeeze of lemon juice

melted butter, to serve

POTATO TOPPING

500 g potatoes, peeled and cut into chunks

20 g butter

80 ml (⅓ cup) cream

salt flakes and freshly ground white pepper

pinch of freshly grated nutmeg

2 egg yolks

This is a souped-up version of a nursery classic. One of the pleasures of eating this is the way the potato mingles with the sauce and changes texture the deeper you delve into the pie, so it's best cooked in a deeper dish rather than a shallow pie plate.

Using three types of fish offers complex tastes and textures: the ocean trout stays soft, while the ling cooks firm, and the smoked fish is crucial for flavour. For me, the inclusion of one-third hot-smoked fish is non-negotiable, but beyond that feel free to choose your favourite fish or whatever looks best at the fishmonger.

If you really want to push the boat out, add some prawns and a couple of mussels to the pie, then serve it with a green salad tossed with mustard & verjus vinaigrette (see page 234).

For the potato topping, boil the potatoes in a saucepan of salted water until cooked, about 15–20 minutes, then drain well and mash with the butter and cream, seasoning to taste with salt, pepper and nutmeg. Leave to cool to room temperature, then mix in the egg yolks.

Melt the butter in a saucepan over low–medium heat, add the shallot, fennel seeds and star anise and cook until the shallot is soft and translucent. Add the vermouth and simmer until reduced to a syrupy glaze. Add the stock and simmer until reduced by half. Add the cream and simmer until reduced to a sauce consistency that will coat the back of a spoon. Add the fish to the sauce and cook over low heat for 3 minutes until just done. Fold through the peas, hard-boiled eggs and herbs. Season to taste with salt and pepper and a little lemon juice.

Preheat the oven to 220°C.

Divide the fish mixture among four individual ovenproof bowls or spoon into a deep baking dish, then top with the mashed potato and bake for 15–20 minutes until golden brown and heated through. Brush the top of each pie with melted butter and serve immediately.

184

SALT-BAKED BARRAMUNDI WITH BRAISED FENNEL

SERVES 4

1 × 1.2 kg barramundi, cleaned, gutted and scaled

1 kg fine salt

1 lemon, cut into 5 mm slices

handful of dill sprigs

lemon wedges, to serve

BRAISED FENNEL

2 fennel bulbs, cut into quarters lengthways

pinch of salt flakes

large pinch of caster sugar

1 tablespoon olive oil

½ teaspoon fennel seeds, lightly crushed

pinch of saffron threads

2 tablespoons white wine

2 tablespoons vermouth

squeeze of lemon juice

2 tablespoons double cream

handful of dill, chopped

1 tablespoon butter

freshly ground black pepper

Braising the fennel with a pinch of saffron adds some colour and a subtle, exotic flavour. If barramundi is unavailable, a similar-sized ocean trout also works well cooked in this way. And if you don't have any vermouth handy, just use double the amount of white wine. A great way to check if the fish is done is to get the fishmonger to keep the dorsal fin on the fish, then leave the first spine from the head sticking out of the salt. When you are curious, gently pull on the spine and if it slips out easily, the fish is ready.

Preheat the oven to 200°C.

For the braised fennel, season the fennel with the salt and sugar. Heat the olive oil in an ovenproof saucepan or flameproof casserole and saute the fennel with the fennel seeds until the fennel is a light golden colour. Add the saffron, wine and vermouth and cover with a circle of baking paper, to help the fennel cook evenly. Transfer the pan to the oven and cook the fennel for about 20 minutes or until tender.

Meanwhile, choose a baking dish or roasting tin large enough to hold the barramundi. Mix the salt with 50 ml of cold water, then press a 1 cm thick layer into the base of the dish or tin, moulding the salt into the shape of the fish. Lay the fish on top.

Place the lemon slices and dill inside the belly cavity of the fish, then cover the fish with a 1 cm thick layer of the salt, moulding it around the fish so it's completely enclosed. Lightly spritz the salt-covered fish with water from a spray bottle – just enough to give a thin film of moisture on the surface of the salt. Bake the fish in the oven for 15 minutes, then remove and leave to rest for 5 minutes while you finish the fennel.

Remove the braised fennel from the oven and place on the stovetop over medium heat. Add the lemon juice, cream and dill and bring to the boil, then turn off the heat and add the butter, swirling the pan to melt the butter and enrich the sauce. Don't allow the sauce to boil after the butter has been added or it will split and have a slick of butter on the surface, which isn't very appealing.

To serve, crack the salt crust with a knife – it should break away in chunks like baked clay. Carefully peel back the skin from the fish, then slide pieces of fish fillet off the bone (they should come away very easily). Serve with the braised fennel and wedges of lemon for squeezing.

BRAISED OXTAIL & CHEEK WITH ONIONS & ANCHOVY

SERVES 4

8 joints of oxtail

2 ox cheeks, cut in half

salt flakes and freshly ground
   black pepper

100 g plain flour

100 g butter

6 onions, thinly sliced into rings

10 garlic cloves, thinly sliced

½ teaspoon cayenne pepper

2 bay leaves

handful of sage leaves, chopped

125 ml (½ cup) dark ale

40 g anchovies, chopped

handful of flat-leaf parsley leaves,
   chopped, plus extra to serve

1 tablespoon red wine vinegar

Inspired by a Simon Hopkinson recipe, this is a great meal for when you are busy, as it needs time rather than attention, and the result is deeply comforting. You can use any braising beef in place of oxtail and cheek, if you like. I often use Guinness here, but any dark ale or stout will work well, as the onions bring a lot of sweetness to offset the bitter flavour. Mashed potato makes the perfect side with this luscious braise.

Preheat the oven to 140°C.

Season both meats with a little salt and pepper and dust with flour, shaking off any excess. Melt a third of the butter in a large flameproof casserole with a lid over medium–high heat, then brown the meats in three batches, removing the browned meat to a plate and adding the remaining butter between batches.

Carefully pour off all of the fat except 2 tablespoons, then turn the heat down to low and add the onions, garlic, cayenne pepper, bay leaves and sage. Slowly sweat until the onions are soft and translucent, then pour in the ale and simmer for 2 minutes.

Return the meats to the casserole, nestling them among the onions, then cover with baking paper and the lid. Braise in the oven for 3 hours or until the oxtail is falling from the bone and the ox cheek is tender.

Remove the casserole from the oven and gently stir through the anchovies, chopped parsley and vinegar. Cover with the lid and leave to rest for 5 minutes. Scatter with the extra parsley before serving.

188

SEVEN-HOUR POT-ROAST LEG OF LAMB WITH ROOT VEGETABLES

SERVES 6

4 carrots, cut lengthways into halves or quarters

4 onions, cut into quarters

1 large garlic bulb, cut in half

salt flakes and freshly ground black pepper

1 × 2.5 kg lamb leg, on the bone

olive oil, for drizzling

750 ml (3 cups) white wine

3 bay leaves

handful of thyme sprigs

750 g medium-sized potatoes

This is one of the handful of slow-cooked dishes I just had to include in this book. Its beauty lies in its simplicity and the fact that it's all done in one roasting tin. And if you don't want to tackle the hasselback potatoes, you can serve it with potato mash.

A great way to break up the cooking time is to do the initial high-temperature roasting of the lamb and vegetables the night before. Refrigerate overnight, then when you wake up, turn on the oven at the lower temperature, add the wine to the tin and bring to the boil on the stovetop, then carry on with the recipe. If, on the other hand, it would suit you better to cook the meat for longer, drop the oven temperature by 10°C and this will give you another couple of hours. When you get home, just plonk the potatoes in the roasting tin and dinner will be ready in about an hour.

Preheat the oven to 220°C.

Place the carrots, onions and garlic in a heavy-based roasting tin. Season the lamb and place on top, drizzle with olive oil and roast for 20 minutes. Turn the lamb and give it another 10 minutes, then remove from the oven. Reduce the oven temperature to 120°C.

Add the wine to the tin and bring to the boil on the stovetop, then add the bay leaves and thyme. Cover the tin with a tight-fitting lid or a double layer of foil, return to the oven and roast, basting regularly, until the meat is soft and falling off the bone, which will take 6–7 hours.

About 1½ hours before the end of the roasting time, peel the potatoes and cut them in half lengthways. Using a very sharp knife, carefully make closely spaced slits crossways almost to the base of each potato half, to make hasselback potatoes. Nestle the potatoes into the tin, placing them fin-side up: the cooking juices should come about halfway up the potatoes; if not, add a little water to the tin. Cover and roast for 30 minutes, then remove the lid or foil and baste the lamb and the potatoes. Increase the oven temperature to 180°C and roast for another 30 minutes or until the fins of the potatoes are browned and crisp.

Serve the lamb on a platter, pulling the meat into chunks using a fork and spoon, and place the veges on a separate platter. Strain the cooking juices into a sauceboat or jug and serve alongside.

APPLE TARTE FINE

SERVES 10–12

100 g caster sugar

100 g almonds, skin on

100 g chilled unsalted butter, diced

pinch of fine salt

2 teaspoons brandy

1 egg, lightly beaten

3 teaspoons milk

300 g puff pastry

6 granny smith apples, cored and thinly sliced

pure icing sugar, for dusting

A pastry masterpiece – thank you, France! This is simple to make, but the oven temperature and timing is critical: an initial blast of heat is needed to set the pastry and melt the butter between the layers, before the temperature is reduced to finish the cooking and caramelise the apples. If the oven is not hot enough to begin with, the pastry won't go crispy on the base, but if you leave the heat on high for too long, the pastry will burn.

This recipe makes about 250 g frangipane; you'll need around 125 g for this tart, but the rest will keep in the fridge for a week, ready for you to use in your next fruit tart – try pear, rhubarb, peach or plum.

For the frangipane, blitz 25 g of the sugar with the almonds in a blender or small food processor until finely ground. Add the butter and the remaining 75 g of sugar, and process until pale and fluffy. Slowly add the brandy, followed by the egg and the milk, mixing until smooth and well combined.

Line a large baking sheet with baking paper.

On a lightly floured benchtop, roll out the pastry into a 3 mm thick rectangle that will fit the baking sheet. Carefully transfer the pastry to the prepared baking sheet, then refrigerate for 30 minutes.

Preheat the oven to 220°C.

Prick the pastry all over with a fork, then spread with a 2.5 mm layer of frangipane. Lay overlapping slices of apple onto the pastry in rows and dust well with icing sugar.

Bake for 10 minutes, then lower the oven temperature to 195°C and bake until the pastry is golden brown and the apples are soft and well caramelised, about 45 minutes. Cool on a wire rack.

192

LEMON DELICIOUS JARS WITH CHANTILLY CREAM

SERVES 6

90 g butter

300 g caster sugar

finely grated zest and juice of 3 lemons

4 eggs, separated

400 ml milk

100 g self-raising flour

pure icing sugar, for dusting

CHANTILLY CREAM

200 ml whipping cream

20 g pure icing sugar

seeds scraped from ½ vanilla bean

There are numerous lemon delicious recipes, many of them family favourites. Essentially, they are all versions of a self-saucing pudding, which works on the basis that the batter below the waterline remains custard, while that above turns to a light sponge cake. This means you can change the ratio of sponge to custard to suit your taste by varying the depth of the water in the roasting tin.

Six 300 ml jars are ideal for this, then you can three-quarters fill them with batter, which will rise to the brim during cooking, but if you don't have any suitably sized jars, simply pour the batter into a baking dish and bake in the water bath for about twice as long. And if you don't want to make the chantilly cream, this is just as nice served with creme fraiche.

Preheat the oven to 160°C.

In an electric mixer, cream the butter and 200 g of the caster sugar with the lemon zest until pale and fluffy. Add the egg yolks and mix well. Gradually add the milk, lemon juice and flour in turns, mixing well between each addition, to make a smooth batter. Scrape into a large bowl, then thoroughly wash and dry the mixer bowl.

Place the egg whites in the clean mixer bowl and whisk with the remaining 100 g caster sugar to soft peaks, then gently fold through the batter.

Divide the batter among six 300 ml jars, then place the jars in a roasting tin lined with a tea towel (this stops the jars coming into direct contact with the hot roasting tin during cooking) and pour in enough hot water to come about halfway up the sides of the jars.

Carefully transfer to the oven and bake for 20 minutes or until golden on top and springy to the touch. Turn the oven off and let the puddings rest in the oven for another 20 minutes, so the custard firms slightly.

Meanwhile, combine all the ingredients for the chantilly cream in a bowl and whip to soft peaks.

Serve the lemon delicious jars warm, dusted with icing sugar and with the soft chantilly cream on the side.

194

BITTER CHOCOLATE & BEETROOT CAKE

MAKES 1 × 20 CM ROUND CAKE

400 g beetroot
canola oil spray
250 g self-raising flour
50 g natural cocoa powder
130 g butter, at room temperature
90 g dark chocolate
325 g brown sugar
4 eggs, lightly beaten
pinch of fine salt
2 tablespoons raw cocoa nibs

The beetroot adds texture, earthiness and moisture to the cake – don't be tempted to leave it out or skimp on the amount, as the high cocoa content means you'll risk ending up with a very dusty and crumbly cake. This cake is delicious served with creme fraiche or chantilly cream (see page 192).

Boil the beetroots in their skins for 45 minutes or until tender when pierced with a skewer. Remove the beets from the water and leave to cool before peeling and coarsely grating. Weigh out 300 g grated beetroot and set aside (any excess grated beetroot makes a lovely addition to a green salad).

Preheat the oven to 160°C. Spray a 20 cm round springform cake tin with canola oil and line the base with baking paper.

Sift the flour and cocoa together into a bowl.

Break the chocolate into chunks and place in a heatproof bowl. Set the bowl over a pan of hot water and stir until the chocolate has melted.

Using an electric mixer, cream the butter and sugar until pale and fluffy. Slowly add the eggs and the melted chocolate, beating well after each addition. Fold in the flour and salt, then gently fold in the cocoa nibs and grated beetroot.

Pour the batter into the prepared tin and bake for 1 hour or until a skewer inserted in the centre comes out clean.

STICKY TOFFEE PUDDING WITH BUTTERSCOTCH SAUCE

SERVES 4

175 g dried dates, pitted and roughly chopped

135 g dried apricots, roughly chopped

2 teaspoons bicarbonate of soda

100 g butter, at room temperature

3 eggs

225 g brown sugar

260 g plain flour, sifted

BUTTERSCOTCH SAUCE

200 g caster sugar

seeds scraped from ½ vanilla bean

200 ml cream

200 g butter, diced

juice of ½ lemon

This much-loved pudding can be cooked in one large mould or tin, or in four 250 ml baking dishes or cups – just reduce the cooking time to 15 minutes for individual puddings.

Butter and flour a 1-litre pudding mould or loaf tin or a 24 cm cake tin.

To make the butterscotch sauce, combine the sugar and vanilla seeds with 80 ml (⅓ cup) of water in a small saucepan. Stir over low–medium heat until the sugar has completely dissolved, then bring to the boil and cook without stirring until the caramel is a deep crimson colour. Carefully pour in the cream – it will spit – then whisk in the butter. Add enough lemon juice to balance the sweetness. Pour 200 ml of the butterscotch sauce into the base of the prepared mould or tin.

Blitz the dates and apricots in a food processor until chopped, then place in a saucepan with 375 ml (1½ cups) of water and the bicarbonate of soda. Bring to the boil and simmer until the fruit is soft, then leave to cool to room temperature.

Preheat the oven to 175°C.

Using an electric mixer, cream the butter and sugar until pale and fluffy. Add the eggs one at a time, mixing well after each addition.

Stir the fruit into the batter, then fold in the flour with a spoon or spatula until there are no lumps. Spoon the batter into the mould or tin, cover with foil and bake for 45 minutes or until a skewer inserted in the centre comes out clean.

Gently warm the remaining butterscotch sauce and serve with the pudding.

196

PEAR & GINGER UPSIDE-DOWN CAKE

MAKES 1 × 28 CM
ROUND CAKE

6 beurre bosc pears or 1.25 kg
   good-quality bottled or canned
   pear halves
12 maraschino or glace cherries
12 walnuts
250 g black treacle
250 g golden syrup
pinch of salt flakes
325 ml full-cream milk
250 g butter, diced, plus extra
   for greasing
4 eggs
500 g plain flour
2 teaspoons bicarbonate of soda
1 teaspoon freshly grated nutmeg
1 teaspoon ground allspice
2 teaspoons ground cinnamon
3 teaspoons ground ginger

CARAMEL
300 g caster sugar
100 g butter, diced

This will turn heads – it looks spectacular, and the combination of gingerbread and pear is divine. Serve with butterscotch sauce (see page 195) and a dollop of chantilly cream (see page 55).

Line a 28 cm round springform cake tin with buttered baking paper.

Make the caramel by adding the sugar to 125 ml (½ cup) of water in a small saucepan and swirling the pan over low heat until the sugar has dissolved. Add the butter, increase the heat and boil the caramel until it is a deep crimson colour – without stirring, or the sugar will crystallise. Immediately pour the caramel into the base of the prepared tin (the caramel will quickly set, so there's no need to worry about it leaking).

Peel and halve the pears, then scoop out the cores with a teaspoon or melon baller. Place a cherry in each cavity.

Arrange the pears in the cake tin on top of the caramel, placing them cherry side down, with their stalk ends towards the centre. Add the walnuts to the tin, using them to fill any gaps between the pears.

Preheat the oven to 180°C.

In a saucepan, combine the treacle, golden syrup, salt and milk and warm over low heat – don't let it boil! Add the butter and stir to melt, then remove from the heat and leave to cool slightly.

Sift the flour with the bicarbonate of soda and spices.

Break the eggs into a large bowl, whisk well, then whisk in the warm milk mixture. Gently fold in the flour mixture to make a smooth batter, then pour into the cake tin over the pears.

Place the cake tin on a baking tray, then bake for about 1 hour or until the cake is well risen – when it is ready, a skewer inserted in the centre should come out clean. Remove from the oven and allow to cool before removing from the tin.

LAR

DER

A well-stocked larder, fridge and freezer are a busy cook's secret weapons. At home and at Kitchen by Mike, pickles, jams, sauces and stocks play a vital role in my day-to-day cooking. With seasonal produce preserved and put away for another day, half the work involved in getting food on the table is already done, which is a luxury in any kitchen, and a welcome time-saving measure in our busy lives. When time is plentiful, you can replenish the stores again – and perhaps try making your own bread, yoghurt and cheese. You'll be amazed at the difference these will make to your meals at home.

BREAD

Bread has always been a focus at Kitchen by Mike. When I first looked at the bewildering list of ingredients on a pack of sliced bread I knew that, for a bread-lover like myself, the only way forward would be to seek out great sourdough from bakers committed to the craft, or make it myself.

True sourdough bread is much more nutritious then 'factory bread'. Not only does the lactic acid produced by the sourdough culture make the vitamins and minerals in the flour easier for the body to absorb, but it also breaks down the gluten in the flour so it is more readily digestible and less likely to be a cause of intolerance. What's more, sourdough bread also has a lower GI or glycaemic index, which means that the carbohydrate in the bread is released into the bloodstream at a slower rate, without causing a spike in blood glucose levels.

I spent years making bread at home. My first loaves were like bricks, but with practice and experience, the bricks turned into bread. I hope the notes and recipes below will help to fast-track your breadmaking from the beginning.

SOME NOTES ON EQUIPMENT AND INGREDIENTS

You'll need a few basic bits of kit:

// digital probe thermometer
// pizza stone (if you don't have a brick oven)
// electronic scales
// water atomiser
// lame for scoring loaves, or improvise by carefully flexing a razor blade and securing it to a paddle-pop stick or wooden skewer
// wooden peel or thin wooden board
// banneton, ricotta basket or loaf-sized bowl lined with a tea towel

WATER

Bread can be made using tap water, as long as it is safe to drink and palatable. If your water is particularly hard or soft, or has been heavily treated with chlorine, I suggest you use bottled water for making bread. I have fitted a filter to my tap at home and at Kitchen by Mike to catch any nasties – this makes the water delicious to drink, and suitable for use in recipes such as bread where a consistent outcome is important.

FLOUR

The friendliest type of flour to work with when making sourdough has a protein (gluten) level of between 11 and 11.5%; however, most shop-bought bread flour is 11.5–13.5% protein. Usually this works well enough, but if you are having difficulties working with your dough, try adding a small amount of general-purpose plain flour (9.5–11.5% protein) to lower the gluten content and help the dough come together a little faster and easier. Wherever possible, use unbleached flour for its nutritional value, aroma and flavour, much of which are stripped out of bleached flour.

SALT

Use good-quality sea salt or Himalayan rock salt for the best flavour and to inject as many nutrients as possible.

LARDER

202

SOURDOUGH STARTER

MAKES 750 G

It will take approximately 1 week to make an active starter culture full of healthy bacteria and wild yeasts. If you find yourself with more starter than you need, you can give some to a friend or freeze it for up to 3 months, then bring it back to life again by feeding it over a couple of days following the method below (start from day three) until it is active and bubbly again.

35 g (¼ cup) organic raisins | 385 g baker's flour

Soak the raisins in 125 ml (½ cup) of filtered lukewarm water for 15 minutes, then strain off the raisin-infused water and use straightaway.

Place 40 g flour in a non-reactive bowl. Add 80 ml (⅓ cup) of the raisin water to the flour and mix well to form a paste. Cover with cling film and leave to ferment for 24 hours in a warm spot (around 20°C is ideal).

The next day, add another 40 g flour and 55 ml filtered water to the bowl and mix well to make a slightly thicker paste, ensuring there are no lumps. Cover again and leave to ferment for 24 hours.

By the following day (day three), the paste may have separated and look curdled, but don't worry – just whisk in another 75 g flour and 115 ml filtered water to bring it back to a smooth texture. Cover again and leave to ferment for another 24 hours.

By day four, the starter should have a vinegar-like smell and surface bubbles should be evident. Discard half of the mixture, then whisk in 75 g flour and 115 ml filtered water. Cover again and leave to ferment for 24 hours in the same spot.

On day five, your starter should be quite lively with active bubbles. Whisk in 155 g flour and 225 ml filtered water. Cover loosely to allow the gases released during fermentation to escape, then set aside to ferment for 4 hours or until very bubbly. Place in the fridge and leave for 12 hours before using.

SOURDOUGH SPONGE

MAKES ENOUGH FOR 2 LOAVES OF BREAD, A PIZZA AND SOME ROLLS

Now that you have your beautiful living starter it is time to transform it into a sponge that will sit in your fridge, ready to be drawn from to make breads, pizzas and so on whenever you like. Every time you use some of the sponge, you need to replace it with fresh flour and water – this is called feeding. You should aim to feed the sponge with double the amount you've used, in equal quantities of flour and water: for example, if you remove 250 g sponge, mix 250 g baker's flour with 250 ml filtered water and add this to the sponge, then leave it at room temperature for 2 hours before refrigerating again. This method will keep your sponge slightly alkaline and give it a sweeter flavour, whereas a more acidic sponge will produce heavier, less bubbly bread.

Sourdough likes routine, so try to mix and feed your dough around the same time each day and you will find that your bread will be very consistent and perform the same way each time. If you won't be making bread every day, discard a 'pretend' portion of your sponge – the same amount you would usually use – and feed it as described. And if you are going away, there's no need to worry, as the sponge will happily sit in your fridge for a number of weeks. When you get home, just fall back into a feeding routine for a few days until the sponge becomes active and bubbly, and doesn't taste too acidic. Then you will be ready to resume making bread. If you want more sourdough sponge, simply increase the daily increments until you have what you need.

300 g sourdough starter (see opposite)   300 g baker's flour

Combine the starter with the flour and 300 ml filtered water and mix very well. Scrape into a 1-litre kilner or parfait jar, cover with the lid and allow to stand for 2 hours at room temperature before transferring to the fridge.

In the morning, your sourdough sponge will be ready to use.

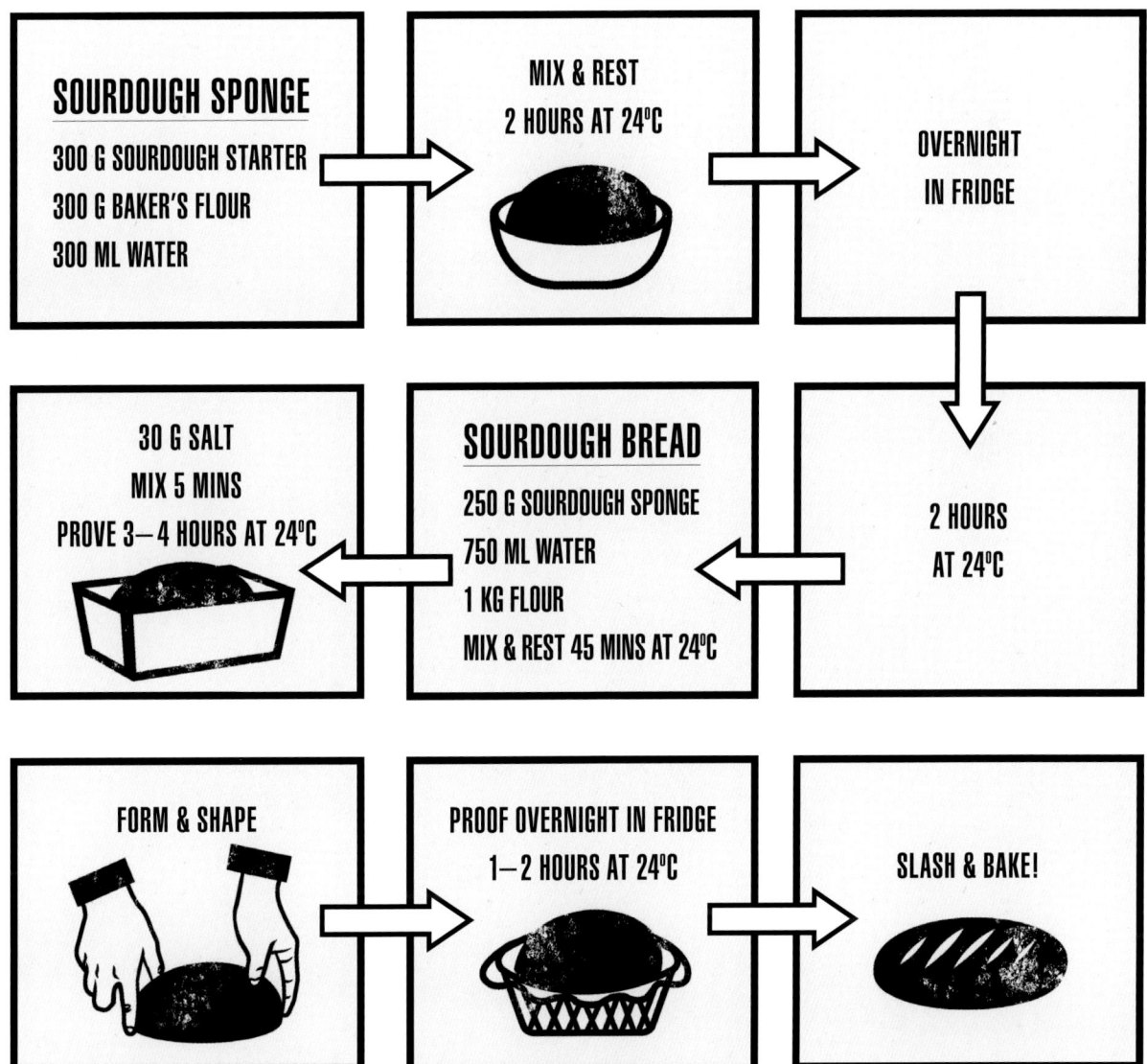

SOURDOUGH SPONGE	MIX & REST	
300 G SOURDOUGH STARTER	2 HOURS AT 24°C	OVERNIGHT IN FRIDGE
300 G BAKER'S FLOUR		
300 ML WATER		

30 G SALT	SOURDOUGH BREAD	
MIX 5 MINS	250 G SOURDOUGH SPONGE	2 HOURS AT 24°C
PROVE 3–4 HOURS AT 24°C	750 ML WATER	
	1 KG FLOUR	
	MIX & REST 45 MINS AT 24°C	

FORM & SHAPE	PROOF OVERNIGHT IN FRIDGE 1–2 HOURS AT 24°C	SLASH & BAKE!

SOURDOUGH BREAD

MAKES 2 × 1 KG LOAVES OR 20 ROLLS

You need to start this the day before you want to bake the bread, as the dough needs to prove overnight in the fridge. If you don't have an electric mixer, work the dough with a wooden spoon and then by hand up to the point of adding the salt. Once the salt has been added, knead the dough until it is elastic and no longer sticky. Fold the dough in half and in half again, then turn and fold in half and in half again. Leave the dough to rest for 30 minutes, then repeat the folding and turning four more times, resting the dough for 30 minutes each time, or until the dough is smooth and glossy. Transfer the dough to a clean tub or bowl and continue with the proving process.

Temperature is crucial when making bread, so you need to monitor it carefully during mixing and proving. If the temperature exceeds 25°C, the lactic acid may change the sugars in the dough, resulting in a flat loaf with a pale crust and a grey-coloured, crumbly interior with a poor aroma.

It's best to bake your loaves on a pizza stone, as a metal baking sheet can cause the base of the bread to burn in a very hot oven.

---

250 g sourdough sponge (see page 202)
1 kg baker's flour, plus extra for dusting
30 g salt flakes

polenta, for dusting (if making loaves)
canola oil spray (if making rolls)

Take the sponge from the fridge 2 hours beforehand and let it come back to room temperature.

Place 750 ml (3 cups) of filtered water (about 20°C) and the sponge in the bowl of an electric mixer fitted with a dough hook and allow to sit for a moment – a healthy sponge should float in water. (If it doesn't, feed your starter and leave at room temperature for 2 hours, then go again.)

With the mixer on very low speed, mix the sponge into the water for 2 minutes, then add the flour and mix for 5 minutes, still at low speed. Turn off the mixer and leave the dough to rest for 45 minutes.

Add the salt and mix the dough on high speed for about 5 minutes or until glossy and coming away from the sides of the bowl. It is important that the dough doesn't get too hot during the mixing – if you can, monitor the temperature with a probe thermometer and stop mixing when it reaches 24°C. This will help to create the right conditions for proving the dough.

Transfer the dough to a clean tub or bowl that allows plenty of room for it to expand, then cover and set aside in a warm spot (ideally around 24°C) for about 3–4 hours.

Once the dough has proved to about 1½ times its original size, it is time to shape the bread.

To make two loaves, tip the dough out onto a well-floured bench and cut in half. Shape each half into a loose ball by cupping your hands around the dough and pulling it towards you, then stretching it into a round shape against the bench. Leave on the bench for 30 minutes to rest and rise slightly.

If you want round loaves, simply neaten and tighten their shape with cupped hands.

If you want oval-shaped (batard) loaves, turn each round of dough upside down and lightly press into a rectangle with your fingertips, then roll tightly into a cylinder, tapering the sides so it looks like a large slug. Place each loaf smooth-side down in a bowl or basket lined with a flour-dusted tea towel. Fold the tea towel over the loaves to cover, then refrigerate overnight.

The next day, about an hour or two before you want to bake the bread, remove the loaves from the refrigerator and leave them, still in their moulds, to come to room temperature. Up-end each loaf from its mould onto a baking sheet or peel dusted with polenta and score the top. The way you do this will influence the way your loaf rises and its shape – I like to make one bold diagonal slash down the centre, because I want a lot of movement.

To make rolls, tip the dough out onto a well-floured bench. Use your fingertips to lightly press the dough into a rectangle, then place on a baking tray sprayed with canola oil. Cover with cling film and refrigerate overnight.

The next day, tip the dough out onto a well-floured bench. Spray the surface of the dough with canola oil and cover with cling film, then leave for 30 minutes to come to room temperature and rise slightly. Uncover the dough, dust with flour, and cut into 5 cm wide sausages, then cut across the sausages to make square or rectangular rolls. Place the rolls on baking trays sprayed with canola oil and leave to rest for 10 minutes or until they spring back when gently pressed.

When you're ready to bake, preheat the oven to its hottest setting (usually about 250°C). Place a roasting tin of hot water on the bottom shelf of the oven to generate steam during the cooking process – and, if you're baking loaves, a pizza stone on the middle shelf.

Carefully slide the bread into the oven (place loaves on the pizza stone and leave rolls on their baking tray), spray inside with a water atomiser and bake for 5 minutes, then spray again and bake for another 5 minutes. Reduce the oven temperature to 210°C and bake bread rolls for another 5–8 minutes. For loaves, spray once more and bake for another 10–20 minutes or until the bread sounds hollow when tapped on the base and the crust has a deep brown colour – a digital probe thermometer inserted into the centre should read 96°C.

Remove the bread from the oven and leave to cool on a wire rack.

RAISIN & WALNUT BREAD

MAKES 1 × 1 KG LOAF

This is a version of the sourdough recipe on page 205, with the addition of nuts, seeds and raisins – feel free to vary these to suit your taste. You need to start this the day before you want to bake the bread, as the dough needs to prove overnight in the fridge.

125 g sourdough sponge (see page 202)

500 g baker's flour, plus extra for dusting

15 g salt flakes

240 g raisins

100 g walnuts

20 g pumpkin seeds

20 g linseeds

10 g poppy seeds

10 g sesame seeds

polenta, for dusting

Take the sponge from the fridge 2 hours beforehand and let it come back to room temperature.

Place 750 ml (3 cups) of filtered lukewarm water and the sponge in the bowl of an electric mixer fitted with a dough hook and allow to sit for a moment – a healthy sponge should float in water.

With the mixer on very low speed, mix the sponge into the water for 2 minutes, then add the flour and mix for 5 minutes, still at low speed. Turn off the mixer and leave the dough to rest for 45 minutes.

Add the salt and mix the dough on high speed for about 5 minutes or until glossy and coming away from the sides of the bowl. Tip the dough out onto a well-floured bench, add the raisins, walnuts and seeds and knead by hand to incorporate.

Place the dough in a clean tub or bowl that allows plenty of room for it to expand, then cover and set aside in a warm spot (ideally around 24°C) for about 3–4 hours, folding and turning the dough every half hour.

Once the dough has proved to about 1½ times its original size, tip it out onto a well-floured bench. Shape by cupping your hands around the dough and pulling it towards you, then stretching it into a round shape against the bench. Leave on the bench for 30 minutes to rest and rise slightly. Neaten and tighten the shape of the loaf with cupped hands, then place smooth-side down in a bowl or basket lined with a flour-dusted tea towel. Fold the tea towel over to cover and refrigerate overnight.

The next day, about an hour or two before you want to bake the bread, remove it from the refrigerator and leave to come to room temperature. Up-end the loaf from its mould onto a baking sheet or peel dusted with polenta and score the top.

Preheat the oven to its hottest setting (usually about 250°C). Place a roasting tin of hot water on the bottom shelf of the oven to generate steam during the cooking process and a pizza stone on the middle shelf.

Carefully slide the bread onto the hot pizza stone, spray inside the oven with a water atomiser, and bake for 5 minutes, then spray again and bake for another 5 minutes. Reduce the oven temperature to 210°C, spray once more and bake for another 10–20 minutes or until the bread sounds hollow when tapped on the base and the crust has a deep brown colour. Remove from the oven and leave to cool on a wire rack.

BRIOCHE

MAKES 1 LOAF OR 10 FLOWERPOT ROLLS

This rich, slightly sweet bread goes perfectly with terrines, parfaits and fruit.

525 g (3½ cups) plain flour
75 g (⅓ cup) caster sugar,
  plus 1 tablespoon extra
30 g dried yeast

5 eggs
115 ml full-cream milk
1 teaspoon salt flakes
180 g butter, at room temperature

Sift the flour into the bowl of an electric mixer fitted with a dough hook, then stir in the sugar and yeast. In another bowl, whisk together the eggs, milk and salt.

Turn the mixer on at low speed and slowly add the egg and milk mixture to the dry ingredients. When all of it has been incorporated, increase the speed to medium and keep mixing for 5 minutes longer or until the dough starts to come together.

Turn the speed up to medium–high and add the softened butter a teaspoon at a time, waiting until each addition has been fully incorporated before adding the next. Once all the butter has been added, keep mixing for 5 minutes longer or until the dough slaps the side of the bowl and comes away cleanly.

Cover the bowl with cling film and leave the dough in a warm place to prove until doubled in size, about 2 hours.

Knock back the dough, then cover the bowl again and refrigerate overnight.

Butter and flour a loaf tin or lightly grease 10 clay flowerpots (or use a large muffin tin) and line with baking paper. If making a loaf, shape the dough into 4 balls, then pop into the prepared tin. If making rolls, divide the dough into 10 and shape into balls, then place a ball of dough into each pot. Leave to come to room temperature and prove until almost doubled in size again (about 2 hours for a loaf or 1 hour for rolls).

Preheat the oven to 175°C.

Bake your brioche loaf for 30–40 minutes, or your rolls for 15–20 minutes until risen and deep golden brown, then remove from the oven. Dissolve the extra caster sugar in a tablespoon of boiling water and brush this syrup over the brioche to glaze.

TOFU, YOGHURT & CHEESE

You'll be surprised at how easy it is to make your own tofu, yoghurt and cheese at home. Cheese-making has been around for thousands of years, ever since people first started to herd milk-producing animals, and with fresh curd cheeses there's no need for humidity-controlled ageing rooms or other specialist equipment. Once you have mastered these simple cheeses, you can trick things up a little by baking or even smoking your cheese – start with the baked ricotta on page 176.

HAND-MADE PRESSED TOFU

MAKES 300 G

Freshly made tofu (see photos over the page) has an amazingly clean flavour and a light texture. It really needs nothing more than wasabi and soy sauce, but it's also good with ginger & lime dressing or black bean vinaigrette (see page 231). Look for dried soy beans, nigari and wooden tofu boxes at health-food shops, or order from Chef's Armoury (chefsarmoury.com); you'll also need a probe thermometer. Although it's best eaten straightaway, homemade tofu will keep in a bowl of water for up to 3 days in the fridge.

350 g dried soy beans	10 g nigari (magnesium chloride)

Soak the soy beans overnight in three times their volume of water in the fridge.

The next day, drain the beans in a colander and rinse under cold running water.

Bring 3 litres of water to the boil in a large saucepan or stockpot. Transfer 800 ml of the boiling water to a food processor or upright blender, add the soy beans and blend to a slurry. Pour the soy bean slurry into the pan of boiling water and cook, stirring constantly for 15 minutes.

Strain through a sieve lined with a double layer of muslin into a clean saucepan, then check the temperature with a probe thermometer. You want to keep the liquid at 80°C, so leave it to cool or place over low heat as necessary.

Mix the nigari with 200 ml of cold water to make a slurry.

When the liquid hits 80°C, stir in a third of the nigari slurry at a time, at 5-minute intervals, stirring more gently each time. In between additions, keep the pan covered and maintain the temperature of the liquid as close to 80°C as possible.

Wait for 5 minutes after adding the last lot of nigari, then spoon the curd into a muslin-lined tofu box. Fold the muslin over the top of the tofu and press lightly for 20 minutes.

Unwrap the tofu, then rinse gently to remove the bitter flavour of the nigari and pat dry before serving.

YOGHURT ≥

MAKES 4 × 125 ML JARS

This pot-set yoghurt recipe was developed with my good friend Pepe Saya, the master of cultured butter. It has been simplified for home cooks and works every time. You'll need a probe thermometer – and remember to allow time for the yoghurt to set overnight and then chill in the fridge for another 24 hours. Once made, the yoghurt will last 3–5 days, depending on how fresh the milk was to start with. Try it with baked rhubarb (see page 51) for breakfast.

500 ml (2 cups) organic full-cream milk

25 g natural active live yoghurt

Pour the milk into a saucepan and heat to 92°C to kill any bacteria. Remove from the heat and allow to cool, monitoring the temperature, until it reaches 37°C.

Meanwhile, sterilise four 125 ml jars (see page 224).

When the milk reaches 37°C, whisk in the yoghurt, then pour into the sterilised jars, filling them right to the top. Seal with sterilised lids, then return the jars to the sterilising pan, arranging them in a tight cluster and adjusting the water level so it comes halfway up the sides of the jars.

Cover the pan with a lid and wrap in a blanket. Place the bundle in a warm place, such as the laundry next to the hot water tank, and leave overnight. (The yoghurt needs to be kept between 20°C and 37°C for 12 hours in order for the culture to develop and multiply.) Once the yoghurt has set like custard, remove the jars from the blanket-wrapped pan and refrigerate for 24 hours to firm up.

LABNEH

MAKES 200 G

Labneh is like a very mild cheese, made simply by draining yoghurt for a time. You can add whatever herbs and flavourings you like. To give it an extra kick, replace the sea salt with the chilli salt on page 228. It can take several days for the labneh to reach the right texture, so start well ahead of time. The good news is that it will keep for up to 3 weeks in a jar of olive oil in the fridge, so feel free to double or triple the quantities below, then you'll always have some on hand.

300 g natural yoghurt
1 teaspoon salt flakes
extra virgin olive oil

small handful of thyme leaves
1 tablespoon marjoram leaves
¼ teaspoon black peppercorns

Line a colander with muslin or a clean Chux cloth. Mix together the yoghurt and salt, then spoon into the muslin. Set the colander over a bowl and leave in the fridge to drain overnight – or longer, if you prefer firmer labneh. Just check it every day until it reaches the texture you like.

Half-fill a small preserving jar with olive oil and add the thyme, marjoram and peppercorns. Spoon small balls of labneh about the size of walnuts into the oil, then top up with enough oil to cover. Place in the fridge and leave for a minimum of 24 hours before eating.

RICOTTA ≥

MAKES 2 KG

Making ricotta is simple and satisfying. Once you get the hang of it, you can play with the flavours and personalise them to your liking. You'll need a probe thermometer to monitor the temperature of the milk, as well as a ricotta basket – ask nicely at your local deli or cheese shop – or just use a colander or sieve (as the ricotta curds are robust, you won't even need to line it with muslin).

Ricotta will keep for a week in the fridge and is fantastic spread on fruit toast and eaten with honeycomb and hazelnuts or walnuts, baked with a citrus-spiked salsa (see page 176), or folded through pasta and salads.

4.5 litres full-cream organic milk	3 teaspoons fine salt
300 ml double cream	juice of about 7 lemons, strained

Pour the milk and cream into a stainless-steel stockpot or large saucepan. Stir in the salt and heat to exactly 85°C.

Add three-quarters of the lemon juice and stir, then gradually add more until the milk splits (you may not need all the lemon juice). Adjust the heat to maintain the temperature of the curds and whey at 85°C for 5 minutes, then ladle the curds into a ricotta basket, colander or sieve set over a bowl to catch the whey. Leave at room temperature to drain for 3 hours.

GOAT'S CURD

MAKES 200 G

Most supermarkets will have goat's milk, but you'll need to source the rennet from a health-food store or online. You'll also need your trusty probe thermometer and some muslin (from kitchenware or fabric shops) or a clean Chux cloth. Fresh goat's curd will keep for up to a week in the fridge, depending on the freshness of the milk used.

1 litre goat's milk	pinch of salt flakes
1 tablespoon rennet	juice of 1 lemon, strained

Pour the goat's milk into a stainless-steel saucepan and heat until it is lukewarm, about 25–35°C. Stir in the rennet, salt and lemon juice to separate the milk into curds and whey, then cover and maintain at the same temperature (25–35°C) for an hour.

Ladle the curd into a muslin-lined colander set over a bowl and let it drain of whey. The longer you leave it, the firmer it becomes. Once the curd has reached the desired consistency, transfer it to a sterilised jar (see page 224) and store in the fridge.

CORDIALS

Because I worry about my children's consumption of artificial additives, foods with e-numbers are banned in our household; unfortunately, this includes most ready-made cordials. Not wanting to be a kill-joy and take all the fun out of eating and drinking, I decided to make my own, so here are three recipes without any nasty additives that will keep everybody happy at teatime, especially with a plate of jammy dodgers (see page 52) on the table.

As the citric acid (available from health-food stores and some supermarkets) acts as a natural preservative, the undiluted cordials will keep for up to 6 months in the fridge. Mixed 50:50 with still or sparkling water, these fruit-based cordials are perfect thirst-quenchers for the whole family. For the adults, I recommend a slug of gin with the lemon barley water. They also make refreshing ice lollies – just pour the diluted cordial into ice-pop moulds and freeze overnight.

STRAWBERRY & ROSEWATER CORDIAL

MAKES 1 LITRE

750 g strawberries, stalks removed
500 g caster sugar

1 teaspoon rosewater
1 tablespoon citric acid

Blitz the strawberries in a blender or food processor until smooth.

Place the sugar in a heavy-based saucepan with 500 ml (2 cups) of water and bring to the boil, stirring to dissolve the sugar. Stir in the strawberry puree, rosewater and citric acid, then remove from the heat and leave to cool to room temperature.

Strain the cordial through a fine-meshed sieve into a jug, then decant into sterilised bottles (see page 224) and store in the fridge.

PINE, LIME & VANILLA CORDIAL

MAKES 1 LITRE

You'll need a juicer to make this tropically inspired cordial.

1 pineapple
500 g caster sugar
100 ml lime juice (from about 6 limes)

2 teaspoons vanilla paste
1 tablespoon citric acid
5 tablespoons liquid glucose

Juice the pineapple – you should get about 400 ml pineapple juice.

Place the sugar in a heavy-based saucepan with 500 ml (2 cups) of water and bring to the boil, stirring to dissolve the sugar.

Add the pineapple juice, lime juice, vanilla paste, citric acid and glucose and simmer for 2 minutes, but don't allow to boil or you'll lose the fresh flavour.

Strain the cordial through a fine-meshed sieve into a heatproof jug, then decant into sterilised bottles (see page 224) and store in the fridge.

LEMON BARLEY WATER

MAKES 1 LITRE

200 g (1 cup) pearl barley
finely grated zest and juice of 9 lemons

250 g caster sugar

Place the barley, lemon zest and 1 litre (4 cups) of water in a heavy-based saucepan and simmer very gently for 1 hour.

Add the sugar and simmer for 10 minutes, stirring to dissolve the sugar, then stir in the lemon juice.

Strain the lemon barley water through a fine-meshed sieve into a heatproof jug, then decant into sterilised bottles (see page 224) and store in the fridge.

218

PRESERVES

Waste not, want not! The long-lost art of preserving vegetables and fruit entails taking what is in season, when there is often a glut, and putting it away for later, when there may be none. If you are on good terms with your greengrocer or stallholders at the market, you can ask them to keep aside for you any seconds that they may not be happy to put on the shelf – with a little trim, many of these blemished fruit and veg will be fine for preserving. Not only does this help to keep the household purse strings tight, but it will also help your grocer move some stock they may not otherwise be able to sell. If you are rigorous about checking the set of your jams and sterilising the jars you use for your preserves, there's no reason why they shouldn't last for at least 6 months. I have some at home that are 2 years old now, and are eating better than ever . . .

CUCUMBER PICKLE

MAKES ABOUT 100 G

This pickled cucumber can be kept for a month in a jar in the fridge, and is great with cold meats and cheese.

1 small cucumber, thinly sliced
1 teaspoon salt flakes

1 teaspoon caster sugar
125 ml (½ cup) Japanese rice vinegar

Toss the cucumber with the salt and sugar in a sieve set over a bowl and leave to sit for 30 minutes.

Pat the cucumber dry, then tip into a non-reactive bowl and stir in the vinegar. Transfer to a sterilised jar (see page 224) and store in the fridge.

LEMON CURD

MAKES 250 G

This will keep for about 2 weeks in the fridge. Use it to make lemon meringue pie (see page 48), to serve with sourdough pancakes (see page 116), or simply to spread on your breakfast toast or afternoon scones.

3 eggs	finely grated zest and juice of 3 lemons
3 egg yolks	pinch of fine salt
110 g (½ cup) caster sugar	80 g butter, diced

Whisk together the eggs, egg yolks and sugar in a heatproof bowl until smooth.

Whisk in the lemon zest and juice and a pinch of salt, then set the bowl over a saucepan of simmering water and whisk constantly until the mixture is thick enough to coat the back of a spoon.

Remove from the heat and whisk in the butter, then strain through a fine-meshed sieve into sterilised jars (see page 224).

MANGO CHUTNEY

MAKES 12 × 250 ML JARS

I never make this at the height of summer, when mango prices are through the roof, but wait until the very end of the season, when they are generally cheaper and seconds are readily available. Frozen mango cheeks will also work, but will produce a smooth chutney, since frozen mangoes become very soft when cooked.

500 ml (2 cups) Japanese rice vinegar	3 tablespoons brown mustard seeds
375 g light brown sugar	360 g (1 cup) treacle
10 mangoes, peeled and cut into 2 cm chunks	150 g (1 cup) raisins, roughly chopped
1 tablespoon ground ginger	1 onion, finely chopped
3 long red chillies, finely chopped	3 cm knob ginger, finely chopped
2 tablespoons salt flakes	

Place the vinegar and sugar in a large non-reactive saucepan or stockpot and bring to the boil, stirring to dissolve the sugar.

Add all the remaining ingredients and simmer for about 1 hour or until the chutney is thick and glossy.

Carefully ladle the hot chutney into hot sterilised jars (see page 224). Screw the lids on very tightly and turn the filled jars upside down – as the chutney cools, a vacuum will be formed.

PEAR & TOMATO CHUTNEY

MAKES 5 × 250 ML JARS

Pears are plentiful in the winter. As they are one of those fruit that are rocks one day, perfect the next, then overripe the day after, there should always be nice pears to choose from. If you want some pep in your chutney, add a couple of pinches of cayenne pepper to the pan.

2 granny smith apples, peeled, cored and cut into 1 cm dice

1 tablespoon salt flakes

400 g caster sugar

1 onion, cut into 1 cm dice

finely grated zest and juice of 1 orange

1 teaspoon ground cinnamon

1 teaspoon freshly grated nutmeg

50 g ginger, finely chopped

400 ml white wine vinegar

4 beurre bosc or corella pears, peeled, cored and cut into 1 cm dice

4 tomatoes, cut into 1 cm dice

80 g (½ cup) sultanas

Place all the ingredients except the pear, tomato and sultanas in a large non-reactive saucepan or stockpot. Bring to the boil, then turn down the heat and simmer for 45 minutes until thick.

Add the pear, tomato and sultanas and simmer for another 45 minutes until the pears are cooked and the chutney is thick and glossy. Carefully ladle the hot chutney into hot sterilised jars (see page 224). Screw the lids on very tightly and turn the filled jars upside down – as the chutney cools, a vacuum will be formed.

PICCALILLI

MAKES 4 × 250 ML JARS

The English version of Indian-style pickled vegetables, piccalilli needs to mature in the jar for at least a month, so plan ahead for this one. Unopened jars of piccalilli will keep for up to 6 months in the pantry and make welcome gifts. Once opened, store in the fridge and use within a month.

Piccalilli is very versatile: serve with a hunk of bread and cheese for a classic ploughman's lunch, in a roll with cured or smoked fish (such as the treacle-cured ocean trout on page 28), or with ham knuckle terrine (see page 32).

1 small cauliflower, cut into small florets

250 g green beans, trimmed and sliced

1 medium zucchini (courgette), cut into 5 mm dice

1 small salad onion, cut into 5 mm dice

1 small red capsicum (pepper), seeds and membrane removed, cut into 5 mm dice

2 corn cobs, kernels cut from the cob with a sharp knife

50 g fine salt

2 teaspoons coriander seeds

2 teaspoons fennel seeds

2 teaspoons cumin seeds

2 tablespoons ground turmeric

2 tablespoons mustard powder

2 tablespoons ground ginger

2 teaspoons brown mustard seeds

2 tablespoons cornflour

600 ml apple cider vinegar

150 g caster sugar

50 g honey

Combine the cauliflower, beans, zucchini, onion, capsicum and corn in a non-reactive bowl. Pour 500 ml (2 cups) of water into a small saucepan, add the salt and warm gently to dissolve the salt. Set aside to cool, then pour over the vegetables. Weigh down the vegetables with a plate or similar to keep them submerged and refrigerate overnight. Rinse and drain, then pat the vegetables dry.

Place the coriander, fennel and cumin seeds in a dry, heavy-based frying pan and lightly toast over medium heat until aromatic, then grind to a powder with a mortar and pestle or electric grinder. Blend the ground spices, including the turmeric, mustard powder and ginger, with the mustard seeds, cornflour and about 125 ml (½ cup) of the vinegar to make a paste.

Place the remaining vinegar in a large stainless-steel saucepan, together with the sugar and honey, and bring to the boil. Stir some of this syrup through the paste to loosen it, then stir the paste back into the saucepan of syrup. Bring to the boil and simmer for 5 minutes or until thickened, stirring constantly to ensure there are no lumps. Add the vegetables to the pan and stir well, then remove from the heat.

Carefully transfer the hot piccalilli into hot sterilised jars (see page 224). Screw the lids on very tightly and turn the filled jars upside down – as the relish cools, a vacuum will be formed. When cold, turn the jars the right way up again and store in a cool place for 1 month before using.

PRESERVED LEMONS

MAKES ABOUT 3 × 500 ML JARS

This is such a simple recipe, and the resulting preserved lemons are incredibly pure in flavour. Use them to make a zingy salsa (see page 176), to place in the belly of a fish before baking or steaming, or add to a stew, such as the tagine on page 90.

12 lemons
240 g fine salt
1 teaspoon nigella seeds

pinch of saffron threads
about 300 ml lemon juice (from about 6 lemons)

Wash the lemons very well to remove any wax from the skin.

Combine the salt, nigella seeds and saffron in a large bowl and set aside.

Bring a large pan of water to the boil, then add the lemons, weighing them down with a heatproof plate or a lid smaller than the pan to keep them submerged. Simmer for 10 minutes, then remove the lemons from the water and allow to cool.

Cut the cooled lemons into quarters and toss them through the salt mixture so they are heavily coated. Tightly pack the lemon quarters into sterilised jars (see page 224), dividing the salt mixture among the jars and topping them up to the brim with lemon juice.

Screw the lids on the jars and keep in a dark place for at least 3 months before using. After this time, store in the fridge, where the preserved lemons will keep for up to 2 years, their flavour intensifying over time.

QUINCE RELISH

MAKES 5 × 250 ML JARS

If you were to ask me what my favourite fruit is, every time my answer would be quince. It generally takes a little work and a lot of time to get the best from them – but if you are feeling game, try a thin slice of raw quince sprinkled with sea salt.

This relish is packed with floral notes from the quince and vanilla. It is very versatile, effortlessly cutting through rich cheeses and fatty meats: serve with cheese or charcuterie, alongside pork chops, or in the pulled pork roll on page 145. Unopened, it will keep for at least 6 months; once opened, store in the fridge and use within 3 months.

1 kg quince
about 1 kg caster sugar
1 vanilla bean, split
2 bay leaves
2 cinnamon quills
5 star anise

2 tablespoons brown mustard seeds
300 ml apple cider vinegar
60 ml (¼ cup) red wine
finely grated zest of ½ lemon
pinch of fine salt

Cut the quince into quarters and remove the cores, but don't peel them. Cut the quince quarters into 2 cm chunks, then place in a preserving pan or a heavy-based, non-reactive saucepan. Cover with 1 litre (4 cups) water and simmer for about an hour until the quince is tender.

Drain the quince, reserving the cooking liquid. Weigh the quince and set aside. Weigh out an equal amount of sugar and place in the pan. Pour in the quince cooking liquid, then add the bay leaves, spices, vinegar, wine, lemon zest and salt.

Bring to the boil, then simmer until the syrup has reduced by a half. Add the quince and simmer until the relish is thick, jam-like and glossy.

Transfer the hot relish to hot sterilised jars (see page 224). Screw the lids on very tightly and turn the filled jars upside down – as the relish cools, a vacuum will be formed.

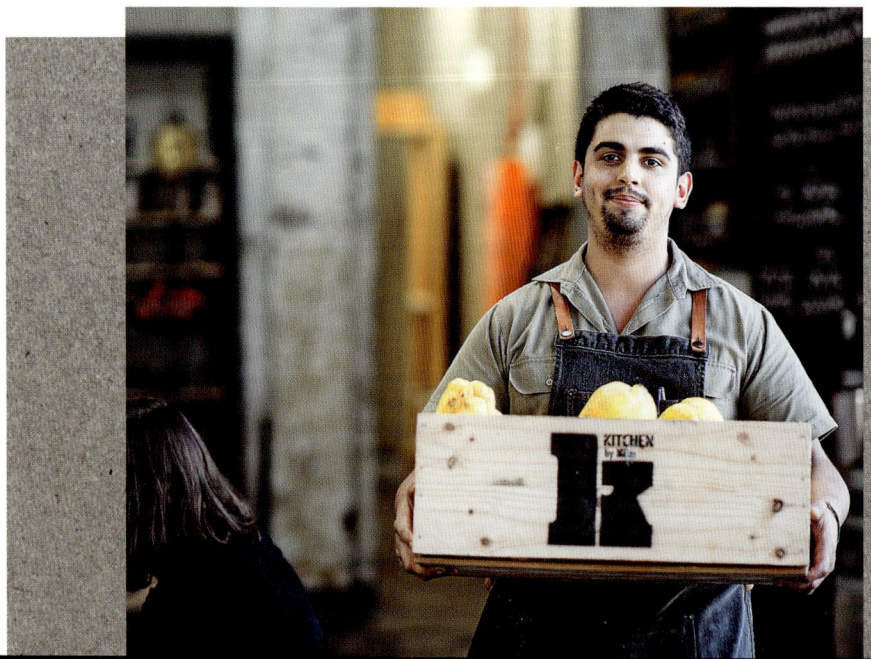

MARMALADE

MAKES 12 × 250 ML JARS

I like to make a large batch of marmalade whenever I come across Seville oranges at the market, as their season is so short and they are hard to find at the best of times. Make sure you ask your greengrocer to order you some. Hopefully, with a little discipline, this amount will last you the year, based on a jar a month . . . Once a jar is open, keep it in the fridge and use within 3 months.

12 Seville oranges	3.6 kg caster sugar

Place the oranges in a large pan or stockpot with 3 litres of water and simmer for 2 hours. Remove the pot from the stove and cover with cling film. Pierce a hole in the cling film to allow steam to escape and leave overnight at room temperature.

The next day, strain the orange cooking water through a muslin-lined sieve into a large non-reactive saucepan. Cut the oranges into quarters and scrape the flesh out with a spoon, leaving as much pith on the skin as possible. Reserve the scraped flesh and pips, as well as the skin.

Place the scraped flesh and pips in the pan of orange cooking water and simmer for 2 hours to extract the natural pectin from the pips. Strain again through a fine-meshed sieve, pushing through as much of the orange pulp as possible, then return 2.4 litres of this liquid to a preserving pan or non-reactive stockpot.

Cut the orange skin into strips (as coarse or fine as you like) and add to the pan. Place the pan over medium heat and simmer until the orange skin is fully cooked and translucent. Add the sugar and simmer until the marmalade reaches 105°C (if you don't have a sugar thermometer, check the set of your jam by dropping some onto a chilled plate – see below).

Remove from the heat and leave to stand for 2 minutes before carefully ladling the hot marmalade into hot sterilised jars (see page 224). Screw the lids on very tightly and turn the filled jars upside down – as the marmalade cools, a vacuum will be formed.

Allow the marmalade to mature for a week in the pantry before using – during this time the set will become a little firmer.

CHECKING THE SET OF JAM OR MARMALADE

The following is a simple way to check whether your jam or marmalade has reached setting point:

// Place a small plate in the fridge to chill for about half an hour.

// Drop a teaspoon of the jam you're making onto the chilled plate and let it cool.

// The consistency of the cold jam is a good indicator of how the finished jam will set. If it is too runny, simmer the jam a little longer and then test again.

STERILISING JARS OR BOTTLES

There are many ways to sterilse jars and bottles for preserving, but this is the method I find easiest at home:

// Preheat the oven to 120°C.

// Wash the jars and a pair of tongs in hot soapy water, then rinse thoroughly.

// Use the tongs to place the jars and their heatproof lids on a baking tray, with the mouths of the jars facing up. Carefully transfer to the oven and leave for 20 minutes.

// Take the baking tray from the oven and use tongs to remove the jars.

// If making hot preserves such as jam, fill the hot jars with hot preserve right to the brim, then screw the lids on very tightly. Turn the filled jars upside down – as the preserve cools, a vacuum will be formed.

// If making cold preserves such as tapenade or chermoula, you should let the jars cool before filling them, and there's no need to turn them upside down afterwards.

QUINCE JAM

MAKES 8 × 250 ML JARS

With its lovely deep rose colour and jewel-like pieces of meaty quince, this is such a pretty-looking jam. It is truly delicious on toast and in muffins (see page 120), and is exquisite with creamy rice pudding (see page 107) or spread over the base of a tart shell and topped with some creme patissiere.

2 kg quince
2 kg caster sugar

juice of 2 lemons

Quarter the quince and remove the cores (reserving them for later), but don't peel them. Cut the quince quarters into 1–2 cm dice and place in a large bowl of water with lemon juice added to stop the quince discolouring.

Place the reserved quince cores in a saucepan with 2 litres of water and simmer for 1 hour – this extracts the quince's natural pectin, which will set the jam. Strain the water into a preserving pan or heavy-based, non-reactive saucepan and discard the cores.

Drain the diced quince and add to the pan, along with the sugar and lemon juice. Simmer over medium heat, stirring occasionally, for 45 minutes–1 hour or until the jam reaches 105°C (if you don't have a sugar thermometer, check the set of your jam by dropping some onto a chilled plate – see page 223).

Carefully ladle the hot jam into hot sterilised jars (see above). Screw the lids on very tightly and turn the filled jars upside down – as the jam cools, a vacuum will be formed.

RASPBERRY JAM

MAKES 5 × 250 ML JARS

Raspberry jam is essential in any larder. It is so versatile and has a pleasing tartness. Fresh raspberries are of course preferable in season, but good-quality frozen berries work almost as well. Raspberries have plenty of natural pectin, which means the jam must be carefully watched as it will set quite quickly – and if you cook it beyond this point, you'll start to lose those fresh berry flavours. Unopened, it will keep for at least 6 months, then for 1 month in the fridge after opening.

1.2 kg raspberries

1 kg caster sugar

juice of ½ lemon

Combine the raspberries and sugar in a glass or ceramic bowl and leave to macerate overnight at room temperature.

The next day, transfer the berries and their juices to a preserving pan or a heavy-based, non-reactive saucepan. Place over low heat and slowly bring to the boil so as not to burst the berries. Simmer gently for about 20 minutes or until the jam reaches 105°C (if you don't have a sugar thermometer, check the set of your jam by dropping some onto a chilled plate – see page 223). The jam will thicken quite quickly once it reaches 102°C, so be careful it doesn't catch on the base. Add lemon juice to taste, then simmer for another 2 minutes.

Remove from the heat and leave to stand for 2 minutes before carefully ladling the hot jam into hot sterilised jars (see opposite). Screw the lids on very tightly and turn the filled jars upside down – as the jam cools, a vacuum will be formed.

FLAVOURED OILS, BUTTERS & SALTS

Having these in your larder and fridge is like having little turbo-boosts of flavour at your fingertips. They can be used for seasoning; in salad dressings; to melt over grilled fish, meat and vegetables; or for pan-frying. Even a little swirled into a sauce just before serving will give it that pick-me-up. With a long shelf-life, these will soon become your new secret weapons in the kitchen.

BASIL OIL
MAKES ABOUT 250 ML

This will keep for up to 3 months in a screwtop jar in the fridge, and is delicious on salads, particularly those made with grains (such as the rice, quinoa, basil and peas on page 23), avocados or tomatoes, or drizzled over fish and vegetables.

1 bunch basil
250 ml (1 cup) grapeseed oil

pinch of salt flakes

Place the basil, oil and salt in a small saucepan and gently warm to 80°C.

Blitz in an upright blender or powerful food processor for 2 minutes. (The faster the blades spin, the finer the basil will be chopped, and the more deeply coloured and flavoured your basil oil will be.)

Strain the basil oil through a sieve lined with three layers of muslin, so you don't get any tiny specks of basil in the oil – these would eventually turn your oil brown.

CHILLI OIL
MAKES 125 ML

Chilli oil can be kept in a jar for 3 months in the fridge and is great for perking up salads, tossing through pasta and vegetables or drizzling on pizza.

1 tablespoon chilli flakes

125 ml (½ cup) olive oil

Place the chilli flakes and oil in a small heavy-based saucepan and gently warm to 80°C, then adjust the heat to maintain this temperature for 5 minutes.

Remove from the heat and allow to cool, then strain into a cold sterilised bottle or jar (see page 224).

CURRY OIL
MAKES ABOUT 125 ML

In a sterilised screwtop jar, this will keep in the fridge for 3 months, and a drizzle is all you need to pep up soups and roasted vegetables.

1½ tablespoons medium curry powder   125 ml (½ cup) extra virgin olive oil

Gently warm the curry powder in a dry frying pan until it is aromatic – watch it carefully as it burns easily – then add the oil and immediately remove from the heat. Leave to cool and infuse for an hour before straining the curry-infused oil through a muslin-lined sieve so there is no powder in the finished oil.

PISTACHIO OIL
MAKES ABOUT 200 ML

The nut content of this oil means it will go rancid if stored for too long, so keep it in the fridge and use within a month – it's so wonderful with chicken or fish and in salad dressings that you'll find it's gone in no time.

70 g (½ cup) unsalted pistachios   140 ml grapeseed oil

Lightly toast the pistachios in a dry, heavy-based frying pan. Transfer to a food processor with the oil and pulse until the nuts are coarsely chopped and the oil is a rich green colour.

RED WINE BUTTER
MAKES ABOUT 125 G

This luscious butter will keep for up to a month in the fridge or 3 months in the freezer, and a slice will add richness and flavour to grilled fish or steak. To make a simple sauce, add a slice at a time to hot stock (off the heat), swirling to emulsify, until the sauce reaches the desired consistency.

50 ml port   125 g butter, at room temperature
3 golden shallots, finely chopped   salt flakes and freshly ground black pepper
100 ml red wine

Place the port and shallot in a small saucepan over medium heat and simmer until reduced by half. Add the wine and simmer for about 5 minutes or until reduced to a syrupy glaze, then leave to cool.

Fold the cooled reduction into the butter, seasoning to taste with salt and pepper. Shape the red wine butter into a sausage, then wrap tightly in cling film and chill for at least 1 hour.

228

CHILLI SALT

MAKES ABOUT 75 G

Rather than starting with whole dried chillies, you could use chilli flakes as a shortcut – just skip the grilling of the chillies and grind the salt with 6 teaspoons of chilli flakes. Or try grinding whole dried chipotle chillies with the salt for a lovely smoky flavour. This spicy salt will keep for several months in an airtight jar in the pantry, and is great for sprinkling on sweetcorn with a squeeze of lime, or as a basic seasoning if you like some heat.

6 dried long red chillies	6 tablespoons salt flakes

Preheat the grill to low. Place the chillies on the grill pan and toast under the grill for about 2 minutes until dark red.

Pulse the chilli in a spice grinder, or pound using a mortar and pestle, to form flakes. Add the salt and pulse or pound once or twice to combine. You can make the chilli salt as coarse or fine as you wish – just blend longer for a finer finish.

FOUR-SPICE SALT

MAKES ABOUT 50 G

This four-spice salt adds the perfect zing to terrines or anything porky. It's also lovely with smoked eel or sprinkled over grilled prawns. Stored in an airtight container, it will keep for at least 6 months in the pantry.

10 white peppercorns	¼ teaspoon freshly grated nutmeg
10 cloves	2 tablespoons salt flakes
1 cinnamon quill	

Lightly toast the peppercorns, cloves and cinnamon quill under a hot grill until fragrant. Allow to cool, then grind to a fine powder with a pestle and mortar or an electric spice grinder. Add the nutmeg and salt flakes and crush lightly to combine.

CONDIMENTS & DRESSINGS

It's such a life-saver to have a range of trusted condiments and dressings that you can reach for at any time to enhance whatever it is you're cooking. And if you make your own, you'll know exactly what's in them – and what isn't (no nasty preservatives, for a start!). You'll also have the freedom to customise the recipe to suit your tastes, and the personal satisfaction that comes with eating something homemade.

AIOLI

MAKES 250 ML

This aioli will give a lift to everything it touches, from its traditional partner of a platter of raw vegetables to the bourride on page 67, or slathered on bread to pep up a sandwich. It will keep for 3–5 days in the fridge, depending on the freshness of the eggs to start with.

2 egg yolks	150 ml vegetable oil
3 garlic cloves, peeled	50 ml olive oil
pinch of salt flakes	freshly ground white pepper
juice of ½ lemon	1 tablespoon extra virgin olive oil (optional)

Place the egg yolks in a bowl. Using a mortar and pestle, or the flat of a knife on a chopping board, crush the garlic with the salt to a smooth paste. Stir the garlic paste into the egg yolks, along with half of the lemon juice.

Slowly, drop by drop, whisk the vegetable and olive oils into the yolk mixture. If the aioli becomes too thick at any stage, thin it down with a teaspoon or two of warm water. Finish with the remaining lemon juice and pepper to taste. If it tastes a bit flat and needs a lift, a tablespoon of young, grassy-green extra virgin olive oil will breathe life into it.

CIDER VINAIGRETTE

MAKES ABOUT 100 ML

This is a simple, versatile dressing for everyday salads.

1 tablespoon apple cider vinegar	1 teaspoon honey
3 tablespoons grapeseed oil	1 teaspoon wholegrain mustard

Whisk together all the ingredients in a small bowl.

GINGER & LIME DRESSING

MAKES 125 ML

A sharp, clean-tasting dressing that goes well with oysters and sashimi. If you can't find ginger vinegar (look for Yamato brand), use the liquid from a jar of pickled ginger instead.

2 tablespoons ginger vinegar
1 teaspoon lime juice

2 tablespoons soy sauce
2 tablespoons extra virgin olive oil

Strain the ginger vinegar through a fine-meshed sieve into a small bowl, then whisk in the lime juice, soy sauce and olive oil.

BLACK BEAN VINAIGRETTE

MAKES ABOUT 500 ML

Bottled in hot sterilised jars (see page 224) while still hot, this dressing will keep for at least 3 months in your larder and is great served with raw seafood, barbecued meats or tossed through a stir-fry. Once opened, store in the fridge and use within 3 weeks.

250 ml (1 cup) olive oil
90 g salted black beans
3 cm knob ginger, cut into fine julienne strips
3 garlic cloves, thinly sliced
1 small red capsicum (pepper), seeds and
    membrane removed, cut into 5 mm dice

100 ml Japanese rice vinegar
75 ml light soy sauce
about 2 teaspoons caster sugar
3 spring onions, thinly sliced

Heat half of the olive oil in a small frying pan over low heat. Add the black beans and saute until the oil turns red and the beans become aromatic. Add the ginger, garlic and capsicum and saute until the capsicum is tender.

Pour in the vinegar and soy sauce and bring to the boil. Taste to check the seasoning and adjust with sugar as necessary. Remove from the heat, then stir in the spring onion and the remaining olive oil.

CHERMOULA

MAKES ABOUT 500 G

Stored in sterilised jars (see page 224) and covered with a film of oil, this will keep in the refrigerator for up to 3 months. It's great to have on hand for marinating chicken or fish and can also be served with crudites or even as a dipping sauce for sashimi.

3 bunches coriander
5 golden shallots, roughly chopped
1 garlic bulb, cloves separated and roughly chopped
15 cm knob ginger, roughly chopped
50 ml extra virgin olive oil
salt flakes
2 stalks lemongrass

1 tablespoon cumin seeds
1 teaspoon coriander seeds
1 teaspoon fennel seeds
1 teaspoon white peppercorns
1 tablespoon sweet paprika
2 teaspoons ras el hanout
½ teaspoon chilli powder
juice of 1 lemon

Remove the roots from the coriander and wash the stalks and leaves well in several changes of water to remove all traces of dirt.

Roughly chop the coriander stalks and leaves, then place in a blender, along with the shallot, garlic, ginger, olive oil and a teaspoon of salt flakes. Blend to a fine paste, then use a Microplane to grate the white parts of the lemongrass into the blender and blend again.

Toast the cumin, coriander and fennel seeds and the peppercorns in a dry heavy-based frying pan until aromatic. Allow to cool slightly before grinding to a powder using a spice grinder or pestle and mortar, then sifting through a fine-meshed sieve.

Add the spices to the blender, along with the paprika, ras el hanout and chilli powder, and blend again. Adjust the seasoning with lemon juice and more salt, if needed.

HARISSA

MAKES ABOUT 125 G

This is my version of the classic North African chilli paste. It may not be as feisty as some, but it is super-versatile. I love it mixed with mayo, dotted on slices of raw fish, served instead of mint sauce or ketchup with barbecued lamb chops, or alongside a tagine (see page 90). If you like it hotter, feel free to add more chillies. This harissa will keep for 3 months in the larder; once opened, refrigerate and use within 3 weeks. To prevent discolouration, re-seal the surface with a thin film of oil after using.

1 teaspoon coriander seeds

1 teaspoon fennel seeds

10 dried long red chillies, seeds removed

1 red capsicum (pepper), seeds and membrane removed, cut into 2 cm squares

80 ml (⅓ cup) extra virgin olive oil, plus extra to seal

1 teaspoon ground cumin

4 garlic cloves, peeled

1 teaspoon salt flakes

Toast the coriander and fennel seeds in a dry heavy-based frying pan until aromatic, then grind to a coarse powder using a spice grinder or pestle and mortar.

Soak the chillies in warm water for 30 minutes until very soft, then drain, reserving the soaking water. Fry the capsicum in the oil until light brown, then transfer to a blender with the chillies and the remaining ingredients and blitz, adding just enough of the chilli-soaking water to form a paste.

Spoon the hot harissa into a hot sterilised jar (see page 224), cover the surface with a thin film of oil to seal and screw the lid on tightly.

HORSERADISH CREAM

MAKES ABOUT 125 G

This is excellent with beef and smoked fish, or tossed through a beetroot salad, and will last for up to 3 days in the fridge.

You can use cream whipped to soft peaks instead of mascarpone, if you like – just make sure you don't over-whip the cream, or it will curdle when you fold it into the vinegar mixture.

40 g fresh horseradish

2 teaspoons Japanese rice vinegar

1 teaspoon Dijon mustard

1 teaspoon caster sugar

pinch of salt flakes

80 g mascarpone

Peel, wash and finely grate the horseradish. Combine in a non-reactive bowl with the vinegar, mustard, sugar and salt, then leave to infuse for 30 minutes.

Lightly whisk in the mascarpone, being careful not to overwork and split the sauce. Cover and store in the fridge until ready to serve – it will keep for up to 3 days.

234

MIRIN & GINGER DRESSING

MAKES ABOUT 250 ML

This super-light dressing is good with any green salad (such as the cucumbers on page 64), steamed vegetables or even oysters, and will keep in the fridge for up to 2 weeks. Whisk in some sesame oil or olive oil to turn it into a more conventional vinaigrette that will lightly coat your ingredients.

220 ml mirin
80 ml (⅓ cup) Japanese rice vinegar
1½ tablespoons soy sauce

3 cm knob ginger, finely chopped
4 red shallots, finely chopped

Mix all the ingredients together and leave to sit for a minimum of 1 hour before using.

MUSTARD & VERJUS VINAIGRETTE

MAKES ABOUT 50 ML

This is my go-to vinaigrette recipe. An all-purpose dressing for salads and vegetables, it is thick enough to coat vegetables and sink into the folds of lettuce. For an old-school treat, spoon it into the cavity of an avocado or use for dunking grilled asparagus spears.

2 teaspoons Dijon mustard
1 teaspoon verjus
salt flakes and freshly ground white pepper

1 tablespoon extra virgin olive oil
2 teaspoons vegetable oil

Whisk the mustard and verjus together with a pinch of salt and a grinding of white pepper, then slowly drizzle in the oils to emulsify into a thick dressing.

ORANGE BLOSSOM DRESSING

MAKES ABOUT 100 ML

This lovely, summery dressing will keep for a week in the fridge and adds a lovely fresh, floral note to any green salad.

30 ml orange blossom water
2 teaspoons honey
15 ml chardonnay vinegar

45 ml extra virgin olive oil
5 sprigs thyme, leaves only
salt flakes and freshly ground black pepper

Combine all the ingredients except the salt and pepper in a small jar or bottle and shake really hard to bring everything together. Season to taste with salt and pepper.

MAYONNAISE

MAKES ABOUT 300 G

A light-flavoured vegetable oil is best for making mayonnaise, as the end-result needs to be slightly acidic and mustardy, and not overpowered by a spicy olive oil. Homemade mayonnaise will keep for 3–5 days in the fridge.

2 egg yolks
1 teaspoon Dijon mustard
2 teaspoons white wine vinegar

250 ml (1 cup) vegetable oil
salt flakes and freshly ground white pepper, to taste

In a bowl, whisk together the egg yolks, mustard and vinegar with a pinch of salt.

Slowly add the oil in a thin steady stream, whisking constantly, to emulsify.

Adjust the seasoning with salt and pepper, then whisk in a tablespoon of hot water to slightly loosen and stabilise the mayonnaise.

PARSLEY SAUCE

SERVES 4

This lush green sauce is delicious with fish cakes (see page 40) or a piece of grilled or steamed fish.

1¼ teaspoons fennel seeds
1 star anise
40 g butter
2–3 golden shallots, diced
500 ml (2 cups) vermouth
375 ml (1½ cups) fish stock (see page 242)

1 bay leaf
handful of parsley stalks
375 ml (1½ cups) cream
1 bunch flat-leaf parsley, leaves picked
generous squeeze of lemon juice
salt flakes, freshly ground white pepper
    and freshly grated nutmeg, to taste

Lightly crush the fennel seeds and star anise using a pestle and mortar. Melt half of the butter in a saucepan, add the shallot, fennel seeds and star anise and cook until the shallot is soft and translucent. Add the vermouth and simmer until reduced to a syrupy glaze, about 10 minutes.

Add the stock, bay leaf and parsley stalks and simmer until reduced by half, then add the cream. Return to the boil and simmer for a further 10 minutes or until reduced to a sauce consistency. Fish out the bay leaf and parsley stalks and discard. Blend the sauce with a stick blender, then strain through a fine-meshed sieve.

Rinse and finely chop the parsley leaves, then wrap in muslin or a clean Chux cloth and squeeze their green juices into the sauce. Stir in the remaining butter and add a good squeeze of lemon juice. Season the sauce with salt and pepper, then finish with a grating of nutmeg.

ROMESCO SAUCE

MAKES 350 G

This traditional Spanish sauce will keep in a sterilised jar for at least 2 weeks in the fridge, and is great with baked fish (see page 130), roast pork or lamb chops, or as a dipping sauce for asparagus spears. Piquillo peppers are available in jars from specialist food shops. For the dried chillies, try Herbies (herbies.com.au) or good delis; large dried red chillies can be substituted – just be careful to avoid super-hot ones or your romesco could turn out too hot and lacking in nutty finesse.

5 dried nora or guindilla chillies

150 ml extra virgin olive oil

1 vine-ripened tomato

1 × 1 cm thick slice of sourdough bread

10 garlic cloves, peeled

5 piquillo peppers

50 g blanched almonds, toasted and ground

50 g hazelnuts, toasted and ground

1 tablespoon cabernet or sherry vinegar, or to taste

small handful of flat-leaf parsley leaves, chopped

salt flakes and freshly ground white pepper

Preheat the oven to 220°C.

Remove the core and seeds from the chillies, then soak them in hot water for 20 minutes or until soft.

Drizzle a tablespoon of the olive oil over the tomato on a small baking tray and roast until the skin has blistered and split and the tomato is soft to the touch. When the tomato is cool enough to handle, peel it, then cut in half and squeeze out the seeds.

Heat 2 tablespoons of the olive oil in a frying pan and fry the bread on both sides until golden.

In a food processor, blend the garlic with the drained, soaked chillies and the piquillo peppers to a paste. Add the tomato flesh, ground nuts and fried bread and blend to a thick paste, then loosen with a dash of the vinegar. Slowly pour in the remaining olive oil to emulsify and keep blending until the romesco sauce has the consistency of mayonnaise. (If the sauce is too thick, add a little of the chilli-soaking water.) Pulse through the parsley, then season to taste with salt and pepper and add another splash of vinegar if needed.

TOMATO KETCHUP

MAKES ABOUT 2 LITRES

My kids love this tomato ketchup, which is great as it means I don't need to buy the preservative-packed stuff from the shops. The ketchup will keep for 6 months unopened in the larder, or for a month in the fridge after opening. A sausage's best friend, this is also the flavour bomb on Kitchen by Mike's much-loved bacon butty – which is simply a sourdough roll, split and spread generously with Pepe Saya butter then filled with fried bacon and ketchup.

2.5 kg tomatoes, peeled, seeds removed, roughly chopped (or use good-quality canned tomatoes)
1.25 kg onions, roughly chopped
3 red capsicums (peppers), seeds and membrane removed, roughly chopped
220 g (1 cup) brown sugar
375 ml (1½ cups) apple cider vinegar
½ teaspoon mustard powder
5 garlic cloves, minced

2 bay leaves
4 cinnamon quills
½ teaspoon ground allspice
¼ teaspoon ground cloves
¼ teaspoon ground mace
¼ teaspoon freshly ground black pepper
2 teaspoons salt flakes
1 tablespoon smoked sweet paprika

Place the tomato, onion and capsicum in a heavy-based, non-reactive saucepan over low–medium heat and simmer until very soft, about 45 minutes. Puree with a stick blender, then pass through a mouli or coarse-meshed sieve to catch the seeds.

Return the puree to the pan, along with all the remaining ingredients. Reduce the heat and simmer for 45 minutes until thick. Remove the bay leaves and cinnamon quills, then blitz the sauce with the stick blender one more time until very smooth.

Carefully ladle the hot ketchup into hot, sterilised bottles (see page 224). Screw the lids on very tightly and turn the filled bottles upside down – as the ketchup cools, a vacuum will be formed.

YUZU DRESSING

MAKES 160 ML

This Japanese-style dressing keeps well for up to 3 weeks in the fridge, and is light and zesty enough to work with any green salad. Bottled yuzu juice is available from Asian supermarkets and specialist food shops.

1 tablespoon soy sauce
1 tablespoon lime juice
2 tablespoons Japanese rice vinegar

1 tablespoon yuzu juice
2 tablespoons extra virgin olive oil
1 tablespoon toasted sesame oil

Place all the ingredients in a small jar with a screwtop lid and shake vigorously.

ROSEMARY TAPENADE

MAKES 200 G

This robust sauce holds its own when paired with strong flavours, making it my favourite to serve with spit-roast or barbecued lamb. It's also delicious with oily fish like sardines and mackerel, or on toast with goat's cheese. Sealed with a thin film of olive oil, it will keep for 3 weeks in the fridge.

15 g salted capers
large handful of rosemary leaves
4 garlic cloves, peeled
salt flakes
140 g small black olives, ideally taggiasche, pitted and finely chopped
25 g anchovy fillets in oil, drained and finely chopped

handful of flat-leaf parsley leaves, finely shredded
2 sprigs of savory, thyme or tarragon, finely chopped
juice of 1 lemon
extra virgin olive oil, as needed
freshly ground black pepper, to taste

Place the capers in a small bowl of water and leave to soak for 5 minutes. Change the water and soak for another 5 minutes, then drain and pat dry.

Meanwhile, using a mortar and pestle, pound the rosemary and garlic with a pinch of salt to form a paste.

Transfer to a bowl, then add the capers, olives, anchovies, herbs and lemon juice. Mix well, slowly adding just enough olive oil to bring everything together. Season to taste with salt and pepper.

TARTARE SAUCE

MAKES ABOUT 150 G

I love this chunky sauce: the crunch of cornichons, shallots and capers offer not only wonderful textures, but also pack intense individual flavours. I always chop my herbs quite finely for this kind of sauce, as roughly chopped uncooked herbs remind me of lawn clippings!

100 g mayonnaise (see page 235)
1½ teaspoons salted capers, rinsed and patted dry
3 teaspoons finely chopped cornichon
1 tablespoon finely chopped golden shallot

1 tablespoon finely chopped dill
1 tablespoon finely chopped flat-leaf parsley
salt flakes and freshly ground white pepper

Fold all the ingredients except the salt and pepper together in a small bowl.

Check the seasoning and add salt and pepper to taste, keeping in mind that the sauce will already be salty from the capers.

STOCKS

A good stock is not a pot of kitchen scraps that have been heavily boiled, but an essential foundation for great broths, soups, braises and sauces – a freezer full of stock is absolutely priceless. While readymade stocks are of course an option, many are thin, with none of the natural gelatine and protein that gives stock made from scratch such a beautiful viscosity when reduced. In my opinion, commercially produced stocks are also over-seasoned with salt. Stock should not contain salt; if you cook with salty stock, by the time you allow for evaporation during the cooking time, you can all too easily end up with something that resembles sea water.

If there's only one thing in this whole book I would advise you to make ahead of time and always have to hand, it would be stock. Even gently simmering the bones left after a roast dinner for an hour or so with just enough water to cover while you are washing up is better than nothing, and will make a real difference to your cooking.

CHICKEN STOCK

MAKES ABOUT 2 LITRES

This simple white stock recipe is perfect for scaling up and freezing, so you'll always have chicken stock to add depth to soups, stews and sauces – it will keep for 3 days in the fridge, or up to 3 months in the freezer. If you like, add some leek, celery and carrot for sweetness, and perhaps a bay leaf and some parsley stalks. Be careful not to cook your stock too fast by boiling it rapidly, or for too long, or it may become bitter.

2 kg chicken drumsticks

Place the chicken drumsticks and 3 litres of water in a stockpot or large saucepan, topping up with a little more water to cover, if necessary.

Slowly bring to the boil, skimming regularly, then reduce the heat to low and simmer for 1½ hours.

Strain the stock through a fine-meshed sieve and store in the fridge. The next day, remove the layer of fat that will have solidified on top of the stock.

FISH STOCK

MAKES ABOUT 1.5 LITRES

Fish stock is not as versatile as meat stocks, and you can often use chicken stock instead – but for a classic bouillabaisse (see page 18), bourride (see page 67) or parsley sauce (see page 236), the lightness of fish stock will make all the difference. Ask your friendly fishmonger for some fresh fishbones, ideally from flatfish, as their skeletal structure tends to be more robust and will hold more flavour and natural gelatine. Do not use bones from oily fish, such as salmon, tuna and mackerel, as their flavour is too strong and their oils will make your stock cloudy. Fish stock will keep in the fridge for up to 3 days, or in the freezer for 3 months.

50 ml olive oil

1 small onion, finely chopped

½ small fennel bulb, finely chopped

½ leek, finely chopped

1 kg fishbones

125 ml (½ cup) white wine

small handful of parsley stalks

3 star anise

5 white peppercorns

½ lemon, thinly sliced

Pour the olive oil into a stockpot or large saucepan over low–medium heat, then add the onion, fennel and leek and sweat until soft and translucent, about 5 minutes. Add the fishbones and cook until firm.

Add the wine and simmer until reduced by half. Add the parsley stalks, star anise and peppercorns, along with 1.75 litres (7 cups) water. Bring to the boil, then reduce the heat to low and simmer for 20 minutes.

Remove from the heat, add the lemon slices and leave to infuse for 5 minutes. Strain the stock through a muslin-lined sieve, discarding the solids.

VEAL STOCK

MAKES ABOUT 2 LITRES

This is the bee's knees when it comes to recipes for brown veal stock, and you can use this same method with chicken legs or lamb necks to make other brown stocks. Because the stock is cooked at a low temperature, it remains crystal-clear, with a pure and intense flavour: it is incredible drunk like tea, or used to make a light soup or something more grand, and is perfect for reducing into a sauce as its purity means it will reduce without any bitterness. If you have a couple of roasting tins, it's worth making double the amount, as this stock is like liquid gold. Store in the fridge for up to 1 week or in the freezer for 3 months. Once the stock is made, the veal meat can be flaked off the bones and folded through a sauce for pasta or put into a pie.

1 kg veal shank (osso buco)
150 ml vegetable oil
1 carrot, cut into fine julienne strips
1 onion, cut into fine julienne strips
50 ml port
100 ml red wine

1 garlic bulb, cut in half
5 white peppercorns, lightly toasted and cracked
small handful of thyme sprigs
small handful of parsley stalks
1 bay leaf
about 4 litres chicken stock (see page 241)

Preheat the oven to 170°C.

Place the veal shank in a heavy-based roasting tin and cook in the oven for about 1 hour or until deep golden brown.

Meanwhile, heat the vegetable oil in a wok or saucepan and fry the carrot until golden and crisp. Remove and drain on paper towel. Fry the onion until crisp and golden, then remove and drain on paper towel.

When the veal shank is well-browned, remove from the roasting tin and set aside. Reduce the oven temperature to 120°C.

Set the roasting tin on the stovetop over medium heat and deglaze with the port. When the port has reduced to a syrupy glaze, add the red wine and simmer until reduced by half. Return the veal shank to the tin, and add the carrot, onion, garlic, cracked pepper, thyme, parsley stalks and bay leaf to the tin, then add enough chicken stock to cover.

Place in the oven and roast for 8 hours, checking every 2 hours and topping up with more stock to cover, as needed. Do not be tempted to skim the fat during this time, as it will caramelise and intensify the flavour of the stock.

When the stock is ready, gently strain through a sieve lined with three layers of muslin, without pressing down on the solids. Discard all the solids and chill the strained stock in the fridge overnight.

The next day, remove the layer of fat that will have solidified on top of the stock and discard or keep for roasting vegetables. Place the stock in a saucepan and simmer for 15 minutes until reduced by half.

ACKNOWLEDGEMENTS

245

This book would not have been possible without the help of so many talented and creative people that I have worked for and with over the years, and continue to work with today.

Special thanks to my wife Joss. We are a team, and none of this would be possible without your absolute clarity and uncompromising support. To my boys, George, Alfie and William, who will always be my greatest critics. To my mum, who taught me about work ethic and that nothing comes easy.

To Neil Perry, thank you for being my mentor – you were the one who turned on the lights. To Igor and Ludmilla and the rest of the Iggy's universe, thank you for sharing your knowledge and for giving me a place in your bakery – you will always have a place in my heart. To Russel and Sasha, for giving me the opportunity to build Kitchen by Mike: your design and trust have allowed me to push the boundaries.

To Jeffrey De Rome, my left hand, and the big daddy in the kitchen, you have made my ideas a reality. Thank you for your loyalty, honesty and devotion to the craft. I cannot thank you enough. To George Hatzis, the holder of the giant pepper grinder, thank you for your loyalty and humour. There is no better gift a manager can give than to make people smile. To Greg Frazer, the strawberry gentleman, your eye for detail and unparalleled experience have kept us moving in the right direction; you are a true professional.

To the kitchen staff, past and present – Julien Nikiel, Kurt Paulson, Justin Schot, Jarryd Sim, Danny Castiglione, Marco Schmutz, Luca Boitano, Ziaul Haque and Ataur Rahman – thank you for your blood, sweat and tears.

To the floor staff, past and present – Tom Harrison, Ben Goritsas, Valeriya Sizova, Shaun Dunn, Monica Antonetti, Dannika Bennett, Peta Barclay, Kira Stawski, Josiane La Chapelle, Ita Ralago, Rachel Chant, Aryadi Pranata, Melisha Williams, Caroline Fougerouse and Angelo Depaz – thank you for being yourselves, and for making the experience at Kitchen by Mike a relaxed and enjoyable one.

To the fabulous Julie Gibbs, Alison Cowan and Emily O'Neill and the rest of the Penguin Lantern team, thank you for believing in me and producing such a wonderful book. It was such a pleasure to write, and I look forward to the next. Alan Benson, you ate at Kitchen by Mike weekly, and became part of the family. When I was asked who I wanted to photograph the book, I knew you were the only photographer who could capture Kitchen by Mike. You got it from day one. Vanessa Austin, thank you for your great eye and deft touch in styling the food shots.

Pierre Issa, aka Pepe Saya, your butter is part of the Kitchen by Mike DNA. My friend and confidant, your integrity and drive have shown me that there is no other way but forward.

A special thank you to all my suppliers and producers: 4 Pines Brewing Company; Alto Olives; Australia on a Plate; Black Gold; Blackheath Firewood Co.; Breakout River Meats; Byron Smith Horticulture and Urban Growers; Chefs' Warehouse; Co Yo; Cooks Co-op; Country Valley; Dean Hastie at Pica & Pica Design; Denim Yoke; Deshel Foods; DessertMakers; E.W.H. Food Services; The Essential Ingredient; Fagor; Feather and Bone; Fesq & Company; Five Senses Coffee; Fountaindale Eggs; Fresh Food Dairy; GJ Food; Green Pack; Hale Imports; Haverick Meats; Host Hospitality; Iggy's Bread of the World; John Susman; Joseph Wines; Joto Fresh Fish; Lario International; Life in a Jar; Lowe Wines; Madhouse Bakehouse; master potter Malcolm Greenwood; Malfroy's Gold; Murray's Craft Brewing Co.; Nicholson & Saville; OVViO Organics; Pacific Organics; Papanui Eggs; Pepe Saya; Pino's Dolce Vita; Plasdene Glass-Pak; Purezza; Ramasa Fine Foods; Red + White; Riedel; Rob Locke, Food Wine Dine; San José Smallgoods; Simon Johnson; Solutions & Innovations; Sticky Chi Co.; Sydney Direct Fresh Produce; Sydney Fish Market; Sydney Markets; Sydney Packaging; Tathra Oysters; Urban Honey Co.; UTR Fabrication; Van Stom Foods; Venus Whole Foods; Vic's Meat; Victor Churchill; Wholegrain Milling Company; Young Henry's; Zesti Woodfired Ovens.

Finally, to everyone who has come to experience Kitchen by Mike, thank you for your support. You have made this book possible.

LANTERN

Published by the Penguin Group
Penguin Group (Australia)
707 Collins Street, Melbourne, Victoria 3008, Australia
(a division of Penguin Australia Pty Ltd)
Penguin Group (USA) Inc.
375 Hudson Street, New York, New York 10014, USA
Penguin Group (Canada)
90 Eglinton Avenue East, Suite 700, Toronto, Canada ON M4P 2Y3
(a division of Penguin Canada Books Inc.)
Penguin Books Ltd
80 Strand, London WC2R 0RL England
Penguin Ireland
25 St Stephen's Green, Dublin 2, Ireland
(a division of Penguin Books Ltd)
Penguin Books India Pvt Ltd
11 Community Centre, Panchsheel Park, New Delhi – 110 017, India
Penguin Group (NZ)
67 Apollo Drive, Rosedale, Auckland 0632, New Zealand
(a division of Penguin New Zealand Pty Ltd)
Penguin Books (South Africa) (Pty) Ltd, Rosebank Office Park, Block D,
181 Jan Smuts Avenue, Parktown North, Johannesburg, 2196, South Africa
Penguin (Beijing) Ltd
7F, Tower B, Jiaming Center, 27 East Third Ring Road North,
Chaoyang District, Beijing 100020, China

Penguin Books Ltd, Registered Offices: 80 Strand, London, WC2R 0RL, England

First published by Penguin Group (Australia), 2014

10 9 8 7 6 5 4 3 2

Design by Emily O'Neill © Penguin Group (Australia)
Illustration on page 203 by Allie Webb and on page 244 by Emily O'Neill
Photography by Alan Benson
Styling by Vanessa Austin
Thank you to Tomkin, Robert Gordon Australia, Golden Brown Fox
and Hale Imports for generously supplying props for the photography
Typeset in Helvetica Ultra Compressed and Trade Gothic by Post Pre-Press Group,
Brisbane, Queensland
Colour separation by Splitting Image Colour Studio, Clayton, Victoria
Printed and bound in China by 1010 Printing International Limited

National Library of Australia
Cataloguing-in-Publication data:

McEnearney, Mike, author.
Kitchen by Mike / Mike McEnearney ; with photography by Alan Benson.
9781921383502 (hardback)
Includes index.
Cooking.
Cooking (Natural foods)
Natural foods
Condiments.
Benson, Alan, photographer.

641.563

penguin.com.au/lantern

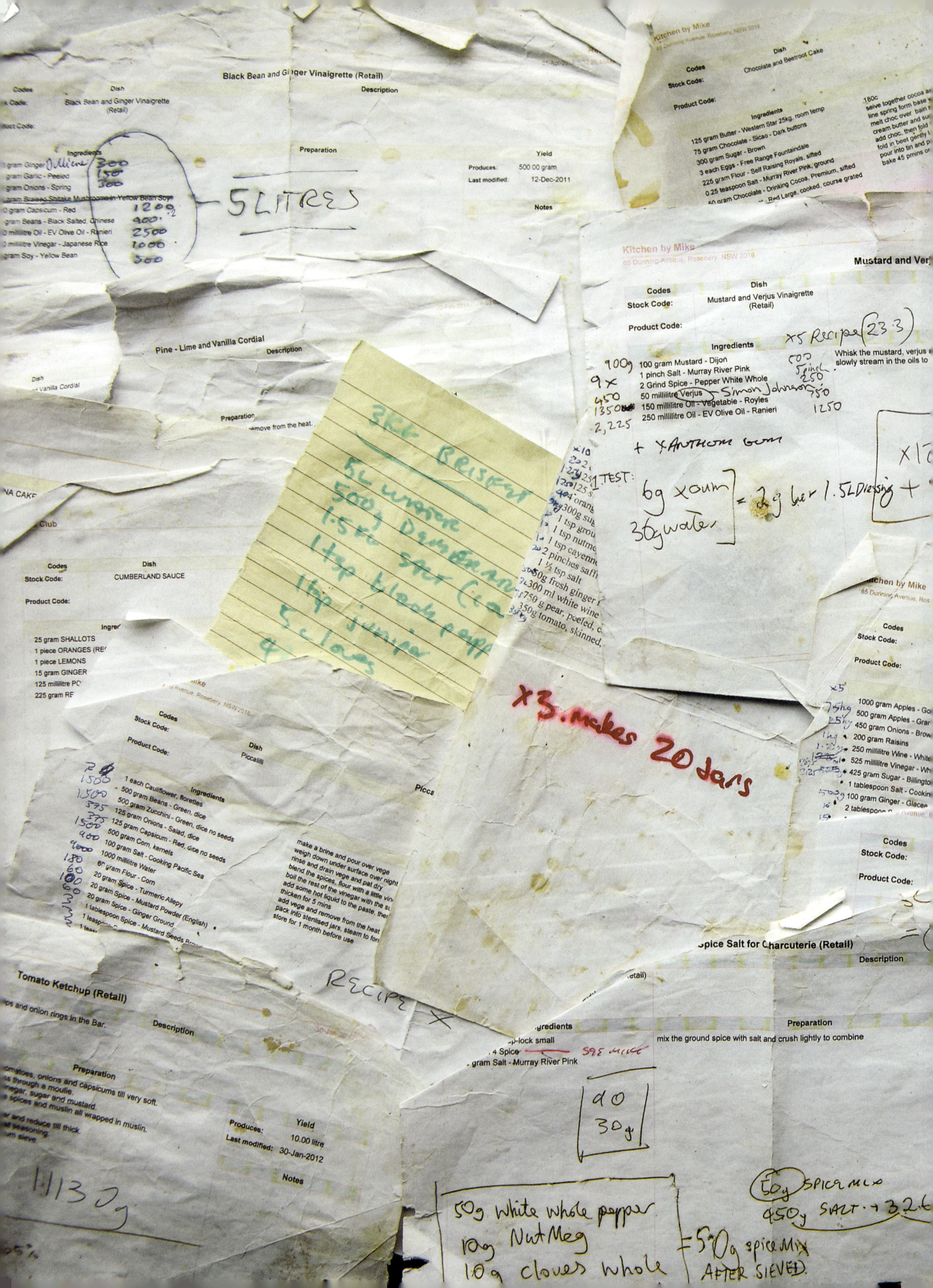

Black Bean and Ginger Vinaigrette (Retail)

Codes | Dish
Code: | Black Bean and Ginger Vinaigrette (Retail)

Description

Preparation

Ingredients
- gram Ginger – Julienne — 300
- gram Garlic – Peeled — 150
- gram Onions – Spring — 300
- gram Braised Shiitake Mushroom in Yellow Bean Soy — 1200
- gram Capsicum – Red — 900
- gram Beans – Black Salted, Chinese — 2500
- millilitre Oil – EV Olive Oil – Ranieri — 2500
- millilitre Vinegar – Japanese Rice — 1000
- gram Soy – Yellow Bean — 500

5 LITRES

Yield
Produces: 500.00 gram
Last modified: 12-Dec-2011

Notes

Kitchen by Mike
85 Dunning Avenue, Rosebery, NSW 2018

Dish: Chocolate and Beetroot Cake

Codes
Stock Code:

Product Code:

Ingredients
- 125 gram Butter – Western Star 25kg, room temp
- 75 gram Chocolate – Sicao – Dark buttons
- 300 gram Sugar – Brown
- 3 each Eggs – Free Range Fountaindale
- 225 gram Flour – Self Raising Royals, sifted
- 0.25 teaspoon Salt – Murray River Pink, ground
- 60 gram Chocolate – Drinking Cocoa, Premium, sifted
- Beetroot – Red Large, cooked, course grated

180c
seive together cocoa
line spring form base
melt choc over bain marie
cream butter and sugar
add choc, then fold
fold in beet gently
pour into tin and
bake 45 pmins or

Kitchen by Mike
85 Dunning Avenue, Rosebery, NSW 2018

Dish: Mustard and Verjus Vinaigrette (Retail)

Codes
Stock Code: Mustard and Verjus Vinaigrette (Retail)

Product Code:

x5 Recipe (23.3)

Ingredients
- 900g — 100 gram Mustard – Dijon — 500
- 9x — 1 pinch Salt – Murray River Pink — 5 pinch
- — 2 Grind Spice – Pepper White Whole — 250
- 450 — 50 millilitre Verjus — Simon Johnson — 750
- 1350 — 150 millilitre Oil – Vegetable – Royles
- 2,225 — 250 millilitre Oil – EV Olive Oil – Ranieri — 1250

Whisk the mustard, verjus
slowly stream in the oils to

+ ½ ANTHOM Gum

TEST:
6g xanthum } = 2g per 1.5L Dressing
30g water

x10

X15

Kitchen by Mike
85 Dunning Avenue, Rosebery, NSW 2018

Codes
Stock Code:

Product Code:

x5
- 1000 gram Apples – Go...
- 500 gram Apples – Gran...
- 450 gram Onions – Brow...
- 200 gram Raisins
- 250 millilitre Wine – White...
- 525 millilitre Vinegar – Wh...
- 425 gram Sugar – Billington...
- 1 tablespoon Salt – Cookin...
- 100 gram Ginger – Glace...
- 2 tablespoon...

Pine - Lime and Vanilla Cordial

Description

Dish
... Vanilla Cordial

Preparation
...remove from the heat.

Dish
CUMBERLAND SAUCE

Codes
Stock Code:

Product Code:

Ingredients
- 25 gram SHALLOTS
- 1 piece ORANGES (RE...
- 1 piece LEMONS
- 15 gram GINGER
- 125 millilitre PO...
- 225 gram R...

Dish
Piccalilli

Codes
Stock Code:

Product Code:

Ingredients
- 1500 — 1 each Cauliflower, florettes — 750
- 1500 — 500 gram Beans – Green, dice — 500
- 375 — 500 gram Zucchini – Green, dice no seeds — 375
- 375 — 125 gram Onions – Salad, dice — 375
- 1500 — 125 gram Capsicum – Red, dice no seeds — 1500
- 400 — 500 gram Salt, kernels — 400
- 3000 — 1000 millilitre Water — 3000
- 180 — 60 gram Cooking Pacific Sea — 180
- 100 — 20 gram Flour – Corn — 100
- 100 — 20 gram Spice – Turmeric Allepy — 100
- 20 gram Spice – Mustard Powder (English)
- 20 gram Spice – Ginger Ground
- 1 tablespoon Spice – Mustard Seeds Brown
- 1 teaspoon Spice...

make a brine and pour over vege...
weigh down under surface over night
rinse and drain vege and pat dry
blend the spices, flour with a little vin...
boil the rest of the vinegar with the su...
add some hot liquid to the paste, then
thicken for 5 mins
add vege and remove from the heat
pack into sterilised jars, steam to for...
store for 1 month before use

RECIPE X

(handwritten card)
3KG BRISKET
5L water
500g Demerara
1.5kg salt (Sea
1 tsp black pepper
1 tsp juniper
5 cloves
4

(handwritten)
x10
300g sug
1 tsp grou
1 tsp nutmeg
1 tsp cayenne
2 pinches saffr
1½ tsp salt
50g fresh ginger
300 ml white wine
750 g pear, peeled, c...
350g tomato, skinned...

4 oran...

---

x3. makes 20 Jars

Spice Salt for Charcuterie (Retail)

Description

Ingredients
- ...ip-lock small
- 4 Spice — 595 MICE
- gram Salt – Murray River Pink

Preparation
mix the ground spice with salt and crush lightly to combine

d0 / 30g

Tomato Ketchup (Retail)

...ps and onion rings in the Bar.

Description

Preparation
...matoes, onions and capsicums till very soft.
...ss through a moulie.
...egar, sugar and mustard
...spices and muslin all wrapped in muslin.
...and reduce till thick
... seasoning.
...sieve

Yield
Produces: 10.00 litre
Last modified: 30-Jan-2012

Notes

1113 0g

(handwritten bottom)
50g White Whole pepper
10g NutMeg
10g cloves Whole } 50g Spice Mix AFTER SIEVED

50g SPICE MIX
950g SALT = 326